Leading
with
GREATNESS!

*Moving PEOPLE and ORGANIZATIONS
from CHAOS and CONFLICT to
COMMUNICATION and COOPERATION*

Jermaine M. Davis

AUTHOR OF:

Get Up Off Your Butt & Do It NOW!

Be Diversity Competent!
*The Art of Understanding and
Communicating Effectively with Others*

COAUTHOR OF:

You Don't Have to SELL OUT to STAND OUT!
50 Professional Women Speak Out

To Cindy,

Lead with

Purpose!

Jeanne

Jermaine M. Davis

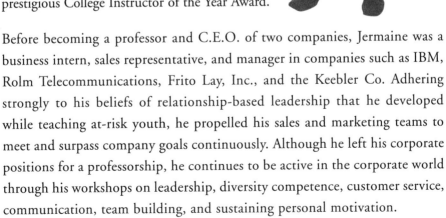

Jermaine M. Davis is the author of four books including the successful seller; *Get Up Off Your Butt & Do It NOW! Staying Motivated Even When You Don't Feel Like It.* He is one of the country's most requested speakers and teachers in the areas of customer service, diversity competence, leadership, motivation, team building, overcoming adversity, and organizational communication. Jermaine is C.E.O. and founder of Seminars & Workshops, Inc. and Snack Attack Vending of Minnesota. He is a professor of Communication Studies at Century College in Minnesota and was nominated by students and presented with the prestigious College Instructor of the Year Award.

Before becoming a professor and C.E.O. of two companies, Jermaine was a business intern, sales representative, and manager in companies such as IBM, Rolm Telecommunications, Frito Lay, Inc., and the Keebler Co. Adhering strongly to his beliefs of relationship-based leadership that he developed while teaching at-risk youth, he propelled his sales and marketing teams to meet and surpass company goals continuously. Although he left his corporate positions for a professorship, he continues to be active in the corporate world through his workshops on leadership, diversity competence, customer service, communication, team building, and sustaining personal motivation.

Jermaine is a Chicago native and presently lives in St. Paul, MN.

ISBN 0-9673500-1-8

Library of Congress Cataloging-in-Publication Data has been filed for.

Manufactured and Printed in the United States of America

First Printing: July 2006

Jermaine M. Davis' books may be purchased in bulk for educational, business, fund-raising, or sales promotional use. For information, please call (651) 487-7576 or e-mail jermaine@jermainedavis.com.

TABLE OF CONTENTS

The Greatest Three 1

Acknowledgements and Thank Yous

Introduction 7

Part One: What is *Leading with Greatness?* 11

Leadership Defined
Motivational Leadership
Inspirational Leadership
Influential Leadership
Persuasive Leadership

The D.A.L.O. Leadership Approach

Part Two: The Importance of Credibility...31

Courageous and Cowardly Leadership

The 5 C's of Building Credibility

Part Three: The Importance of Trust 49

What is Trust, Exactly?

Practical Ideas for Building, Creating, and Earning Trust as a Leader

Regaining Trust as a Leader when Trust is Lost
Hubris: Dangerous and Destructive Leadership
The 5 Steps to Regaining Trust

Part Four: What Do Others Expect of You as a Leader? 67

    Diverse Leadership Styles
        Autocratic Leadership
        Democratic Leadership
        Laissez-Faire Leadership
        Which Leadership Style is Best?

    Are you the Right Match for the Leadership Position?

    The P.V.G. Theory
        Purpose
        Vision
        Goals

    Leading a Team: The Benefits and the Headaches

Part Five: Leadership and Communication 93

    Why is Communication so Important?

    How Does One Communicate Effectively?

    Effective Communication and Leadership Strategies
        The Excellent Communication Philosophy
        The C.P.R. Communication Model

    Barriers to Effective Communication and Leadership

    Learning to Agree to Disagree—Is it Really Possible?

    Emotional Intelligence: Above All, Know Thyself

    The Four Communication Styles
        Passive Style
        Aggressive Style
        Passive-Aggressive Style
        Assertive Style
        Which Communication Style is Best?

Part Six: Handling and Resolving Conflict as a Leader 137

Constructive Conflict

Destructive Conflict

    The 3 Nasty Evils of Destructive Conflict

        Conflict Avoidance

        Conflict Denial

        Conflict Minimization

Preparing to Deal with Conflict

    Know Thyself

    Know Thy Goals

    Know the Other Person(s)

    Know the Communication Context

    Know the Most Appropriate Style

What's All the Fuss About? Types of Conflict

    Substantive Conflict

    Procedural Conflict

    Interpersonal Conflict

Weak Links

    The 3 A's of Weak Links: Abilities, Actions, and Attitudes

    The 5 R's of Helping Weak Links Succeed

The 4 Conflict Resolution Methods

    Lose-Lose

    Win-Lose

    Compromise

    Win-Win

The Bottom Line of Conflict Resolution and *Leading with Greatness*

Finale: Final Thoughts on *Leading with Greatness* 175

Jermaine M. Davis' Biography 180

A Special Invitation from the Author..181

The
Greatest
Three

This book is dedicated to the three women I think about most often: my mother, Carolyn "Charmaine" Davis; my little sister, Katrina Davis-Williams; and my grandmother, Margaret Ann Davis (The Old Girl).

To My Mother,

WE DID IT AGAIN!

You left us physically Friday July 1, 2005, at 3:11 pm, but your aura, ambiance, and presence are still felt. I made a promise at your home-going celebration that your words of wisdom would live through my life, speeches, and writings. Well guess what, ma—I'm fulfilling my promise with this book. I think of you *all* the time and I keep you close to my heart by singing your favorite songs and dancing to the cuts and jams we both liked too listen to when you were here. Making you a proud mother is one of my key motivators and secrets to success. I wish you were here to see your son use his God-given T.A.G.S. (Talents, Abilities, Gifts, and Skills). I know that you're watching, smiling, crying, and laughing wherever you are.

I was thinking the other day, ma...who would have ever thought a little nappy-headed, young black kid, raised in the housing project and slums of Chicago's west-side, would grow up to be an author, business-owner, college professor,

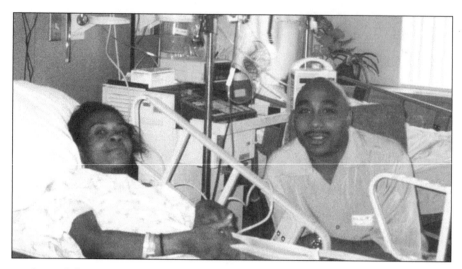

teacher of the year, and professional speaker? According to some statistics and sociologists, I was doomed to fail. However, they didn't factor into the equation your relentless love as a single parent and your unwavering belief in me. You wanted me to succeed, and you told me so, time and time again. When I was younger, your constant advice annoyed me, and I dreaded our heart-to-heart talks at the kitchen table, but now, I see you were only trying to set me up for a successful life! Thanks, ma! I will forever honor you and what you've taught me. I can't wait to see you again!

Oh, yeah! I need a hug!

Your Son, J.D.

*   *   *

To Katrina (my little sister and my little love),

I was 17 years young when I left home for college and you were 9 months young. I had always wanted a little sister—and 16 years later, you were born. I was afraid when I was away in college that, you and I would never develop that true sister and brother love, but boy, was I wrong. Whenever I see you, I become overwhelmed with joy and excitement. You've experienced a lot of hardship lately, but

know and understand that your big brother J.D. will always be there when you need him. I hurt when you hurt, and I feel your pain, believe me. I will walk step-by-step and hand-in-hand with you because I want the best for you. Yes, I will still tell you the truth (Ha! Ha!), but I promise to do it gently and respectfully. Let's make Ma and Lil' Greg proud of us.

I appreciate when you call me and say, "J.D., I love you." Those words have a way of breaking me down emotionally. I love you, too!

Oh, yeah—by the way, Katrina, I can still dance better than you!

Love, Your Big Brother, J.D.

                    *   *   *

To my grandmother (The Old Girl),

WOW! There's so much to thank you for, and I guess I should start by saying this: Thank you for modeling (and teaching me) how to be "an authentic and real person." You've always encouraged me to be me. I remember when you once told me, "Jermaine, I don't know how to do phony well." That phrase has helped me show the world who I am, and I'm still learning to be comfortable in my own skin. Thank you for being the catalyst behind me being *me*. Thank you for introducing me to spirituality and for teaching me how to study and search for truth. Once again, you were the catalyst behind my desire to be a truth-seeker. I love it when my new ideas and insights excite you. I love that you respect me as a person and not just as your grandson. Thank you for being open, honest, and direct with me. You've taught me great things throughout life, and I thank you for being real with me.

Love, Your Grandson, J.D.

*   *   *

ACKNOWLEDGEMENTS AND THANK YOUS

I would like to happily and respectfully thank all the editors who worked extremely hard and diligently on this book and project to ensure its success. I always tell my family members and friends, "Never, ever write a book if you can't handle feedback." I believe writing a book and receiving honest feedback from editors is one of the most humbling experiences. Thank you all for helping me to articulate and communicate effectively my beliefs, emotions, and ideas around relationship-based leadership. Thank you for sharing your T.A.G.S. (Talents, Abilities, Gifts, and Skills) with me. I would like to personally thank:

Chris Traxler, thank you for being a great listener and going out of your way to meet me at Barnes & Noble to complete this book. You worked many late hours on this project and you met and catered to my deadlines. You are a great note-taker, and you helped from the beginning.

Mary Ellen Butler, out on the west coast, in California, thank you for helping me organize my thoughts more effectively. You really helped me when you challenged me to think and write more clearly on the topic of influential and persuasive leadership. I love how gentle you were when you provided me with feedback.

Trish Wooldridge, out on the east coast, in Massachusetts, thank you for really, really pushing me and helping me to bring my best ideas forth. WOW! You and

I have disagreed about all sorts of things regarding this book, but I knew you were only helping me. Thanks for being courageous and for following your beliefs. I have learned to agree to disagree with this project. Thanks for attending my presentations when I was in the Boston area. Thanks for sacrificing and making a commitment to this project; that means a lot to me.

Laurel Hagge, I just love working with you because you are fast, gentle, meticulous, and professional. You did such an excellent job on the first book that I had to include you on this book. Thanks for working around my crazy, hectic, and unpredictable schedule. Thank you for meeting me at Barnes & Noble, Caribou Coffee, and the Chinese restaurant to get this book done. Thanks for being a great colleague at Century College.

Nate Rudd, thanks for doing an awesome job on the front and back cover of the book. You were meticulous and deliberate about your ideas. Thanks for being a fast but quality book cover designer.

Katie Ruberto (a.k.a., M.B.A. Katie), to my friend, colleague, and co-author, I just want you to know that I think you are AWESOME! Thank you so much for your time, participation, and commitment to this project. You were there for me when I experienced writer's block and deep frustration. You encouraged me and pushed me, even, when I didn't feel like writing anymore or editing my own work. You made personal and professional sacrifices because you believe in me and this project. Your project management skills and attention to detail allowed me to see errors I would have overlooked; thank you. I will always cherish the moment when you were in New York editing *Leading with Greatness* and you text-messaged me that "*Leading with Greatness* is a masterpiece." I needed that ego-food at the time and I just want to say thanks again for supporting me both personally and professionally.

Dr. Julie M. Thompson (a.k.a., Dr. Jules) Thanks! Thanks! And, Thanks! You have been a huge inspiration for me professionally. Thanks for your editing contributions to this body of work. I admire the passion and zest you exude as an educator. You inspire me to be the best educator I can be as well. I love your appreciation of hip-hop, jazz, and rhetorical studies. Thank you, again!

Christina Frieler, extremely talented, hardworking, easy going, easy to work with, and diligent are just a few adjectives to describe you. You made this project a huge success and I would like for the whole world to know. Thank you so much for sharing your creative and innovative ideas with me. I will forever remember your sacrifices.

The scripture says, "Give honor unto whom honor is due." I would like to thank once again all the editors who have given of themselves personally and professionally to assist me with my vision for *Leading with Greatness.*

*   *   *

I would like to thank all my family members and friends who supported me emotionally, mentally, physically, professionally, and spiritually during the period I was working on and writing *Leading with Greatness*:

Gregory "Lil' Greg" Davis; Ernest Davis, Jr.; Michael Davis; Kenny Davis; Russel Eliowa Andrae' Dobbey; Russel Dobbey Sr.; Celocia Dobbey; Destin Dobbey; Chelsea "Clint" Frederickson; Herbert Grace; Darrin Green; Tumchee Howard; Jennifer Marah, William Thomas McCreary; Terry Phillips; Alando Randolph; Chester Randolph; Jennifer Randolph; Pat Randolph; Tanya Reiger; Katie Ruberto; Kim Van Swol; Gregory Williams.

Moving People and Organizations from Chaos and Conflict to Communication and Cooperation

A fter leading several workshops and facilitating a three-day communication, conflict resolution, leadership, and team-building retreat in Boise, Idaho, I was in a book store at the airport searching for reading material to occupy my two-hour and forty-three minute flight back to Minneapolis/St. Paul. The wall full of books and magazines overwhelmed me, so I took my time reviewing the selection. I finally chose the last copy of *U.S. News & World Report* special issue titled "America's Best Leaders." Since I had just spent the last three days coaching and facilitating around the topic of leadership, I wanted to see if my ideas were compatible with those the magazine outlined. Minutes after takeoff, I came across two striking statistics that confirmed the premise for the ideas I had recently shared with the organization in Boise, Idaho and that had sparked the origination for *Leading with Greatness.*

The article statistics read, "58% of most leaders in this country today cannot be trusted," and "73% of most leaders in this country are out of touch with the average person." After I read the statistics, I put the magazine down and began to meditate on what they meant to me and to my work. I concluded from the magazine article that the ideas written in this book are needed now more than ever before. The statistics communicated to me that people need to connect personally with and trust their leaders before they can comfortably follow them.

I learned many years ago that colleagues and employees follow leaders they respect and trust and with whom they've built and developed personal and professional relationships.

Yes, this is another leadership book! However, all leadership books are not inspired, written, and created equally. *Leading with Greatness* offers a different twist and a new approach to leading others effectively. The core foundation of this book is what I call relationship-based leadership (also known as the RBL Approach to effective leadership). ***Relationship-based leadership occurs when a leader deliberately establishes and builds interpersonal relationships with their colleagues and employees before attempting to lead them.*** In companies and organizations around the world, people are scrambling to understand why some leaders are more successful than others and how they can mimic the best leadership behaviors. Additionally, leadership theorists and practitioners continue to debate which strategies are more effective when dealing with difficult colleagues and employees.

I believe that great leadership begins with building great relationships. It sounds simple, but many leaders fail because they do not create healthy, open, and trusting work environments in which colleagues and employees will thrive both personally and professionally. Failing leaders are unsuccessful at creating, cultivating, and nurturing strong relationships with their colleagues and employees. Such failure makes it difficult to accomplish the organization's purpose, vision, and goals on a daily basis. Successful organizations need all its employees to work together synergistically; it is imperative that leaders never forget that great leadership begins with great relationships.

It is difficult for colleagues and employees to follow leaders they cannot trust or leaders that cannot relate to the personal and professional life experiences of others. The inability to build trust and to connect with colleagues and employees is a relationship-based issue and a problem many leaders face. A leader that takes the time to understand, respect, and value her or his colleagues and employees is a leader who will ultimately achieve success. Thus, *Leading with Greatness* is all about relationship-based leadership. Leaders must deliberately establish and build interpersonal relationships with their colleagues and employees before they can effectively motivate, inspire, and influence them to achieve organizational goals.

Leaders don't have to be omniscient, but they do have to build trusting relationships and get to know their colleagues and employees if they want to help them achieve the organization's purpose, vision, and goals. Please, don't misunderstand me or misconstrue my message. As a leader, I know dealing with difficult and diverse people can be challenging at times for anyone. Being in a leadership position is probably one of the most daunting and difficult challenges a person will ever experience in her or his professional career. Still, *Leading with Greatness* doesn't have to be physically taxing, emotionally overwhelming, or mentally draining.

Leading with Greatness is about understanding, getting along with, and connecting to the individuals you are leading. When you build great relationships with colleagues and employees, it is easy for them to follow your lead. On the other hand, when you have mediocre relationships with colleagues and employees, it is difficult for them to follow your lead. When you have horrible relationships with colleagues and employees, they may NEVER follow your lead. Ask yourself what kind of relationships are you building with your colleagues and employees every single day? Leadership becomes much easier in an environment where healthy work relationships are established, nurtured, and strengthened regularly.

The ideas written in this book are based on authentic work-related issues and confirmed with real-life experiences. I have also included a series of thought provoking questions to guide and support you on your leadership exploration and journey. Whether you are new to leadership, have a few years of experience, or are a seasoned leader, this book will equip you with the correct tools to become a relationship-based leader by helping you build stronger teams and powerful relationships with the individuals you are leading. These ideas are both priceless and timeless and must be practiced and developed into new habits so that you can lead with greatness and truly move your organization forward.

Now, the questions still remain: Will you or won't you relate to your colleagues and employees? Will you or won't you build lasting, effective, and sustainable relationships with your colleagues and employees? Will you or won't you achieve the goals of your company, institution, or organization? Will you or won't you use relationship-based leadership to effectively lead your team or organization? You must wrestle cognitively and emotionally with these difficult questions if you desire to lead with greatness!

PART ONE

What is
Leading with Greatness?

Are Leaders Born, Made, or Both?

Some people believe those who lead with greatness are innately gifted with the qualities necessary for leadership. The Trait Theory (sometimes called the "Great Woman or Great Man" Theory) states that some individuals are born naturally with certain attributes, characteristics, and qualities that equip them to lead more effectively than others. The problem with this paradigm is that there are no certainties or guarantees that individuals possessing these specific attributes, characteristics, and qualities will be effective leaders. Others believe anyone can lead effectively if she or he is in the right environment at the right time, under the right circumstances, and in the right situation. Situational leaders adjust their leadership styles from context to context, situation to situation, and organization to organization. The Situational Theory of Leadership states that great leaders are not born, but rather are clearly made and developed in the actual environment in which they lead.

My hope and desire is that, after reading *Leading with Greatness*, you will embrace the Situational Theory and realize that learning how to become a relationship-based leader is both a possibility and an achievable reality. Even so-called "born leaders" can use the information in this book to maximize and cultivate their natural T.A.G.S. (Talents, Abilities, Gifts, and Skills as I define them, which I will reference throughout the book) to benefit their colleagues, their employees, their organizations, and themselves. There is a leader in all of us, and with knowledge, confidence, and human relationship skills, you, too, can lead with greatness!

Are You Fit for Leadership?

Don't panic! If you find yourself overwhelmed by the following questions, it simply means you've chosen the right book to help you grow and develop as a leader. These questions will help you decide what kind of leader you want to be and how you plan to get there. Reflect on these questions now and as you continue to read the book regarding your leadership potential:

Would you follow yourself?

Why would you follow yourself?

Why wouldn't you follow yourself?

Take a moment to think about and reflect on these questions. You may realize you already have positive attributes and qualities to bring to a leadership position. You might also find aspects of your leadership style that need to be revamped, revised, and developed so that you can be the kind of leader you want to be or the type of leader your organization needs you to be. Either way, there are always new, better, and more effective skills to learn in order to become a relationship-based leader.

LEADERSHIP DEFINED

Whether natural (Trait Theory) or cultivated (Situational Theory), leaders share a common definition of the core of leadership. They recognize that *leadership is the ability to motivate, inspire, and influence team members to accomplish agreed-upon goals.* Within many organizations, the agreed-upon goals are created from mission and vision statements as well as from departmental objectives, initiatives, and aspirations, and it is important to take a look at each one of these items. At the same time, through using the three main components of leadership—motivation, inspiration, and influence—you can lead your team to help you become even more successful.

Motivational Leadership

Motivation is an external or internal need or want that causes or energizes a person to take action. Motivation is the drive each colleague and employee needs each and every day in order to accomplish personal and organizational goals. Learning what motivates you and others can be complicated at times, yet it is one of the most important keys to *Leading with Greatness*. It is *imperative* that leaders learn what motivates the people with whom they work. It is important that leaders truly understand and accept that colleagues and employees are motivated for their own reasons—not for the reasons of their leaders. All colleagues and employees are motivated in different ways. When leaders embrace this idea, they will find motivating colleagues and employees much easier. You might *never* achieve or accomplish personal and organizational goals if you don't know how to motivate your colleagues and employees. While every leader enters a meeting with what motivates *her* or *him*, she or he then faces a room full of colleagues and employees who have come with their own personal and professional needs and wants that must be affirmed in order for them to sustain motivation. *A great leader never attempts to motivate others from the perspective of her or his own individual motivations.* Instead, a great leader motivates from the perspective of the colleague and employee. As a relationship-based leader, you need to find ways to become familiar with your colleagues and employees and understand what motivates them along with what T.A.G.S. (Talents, Abilities, Gifts, and Skills) they bring to the organization.

For example, you might have an outstanding employee who is struggling because she or he really wants to spend more time with her or his family. You can increase her or his motivation simply by being willing to explore options with her or him, such as allowing her or him to adopt a flexible working schedule, which could consist of an early or late start, a four-day work week consisting of four ten-hour days, or job-sharing opportunities. Using these approaches with each team member can help you assist her or him by drawing on her or his own motivations and allowing her or him to be enthusiastic about reaching the team and organization's collective goals. Because the individual's goals are being met, the individual is more willing to work towards the organization's collective goals. In other words, these approaches help leaders provide an opportunity for colleagues and employees to create a sense of ownership in the organization.

I recently read an article in *FORTUNE* Magazine entitled, "GET A LIFE! The 24/7 Grind Hurts—But Corporations Are Helping Executives Escape It," and it explained that companies who want to attract, recruit, and *retain* the greatest talent for their organizations must understand what motivates each and every single employee. Not knowing what motivates colleagues and employees is not an option for leaders anymore; the days of having employees who are just happy to be employed are gone! The more competent and talented the employees, the higher their expectations are that leaders will address their personal and professional needs, wants, and expectations. The article also addressed the work/life balance issues that challenge many organizations consistently. Companies lose great talent because of lost motivation, burnout, exhaustion, limited family time, ridiculous work schedules, and long hours.

In a poll of male executives, 48% agreed strongly and 36% agreed somewhat that they would like job options that let them realize their professional aspirations while having more time for family, community, religious activities, friends, and hobbies. These statistics reveal that there are many factors that motivate hard-working employees besides money and financial gain. If companies want to keep loyal employees, they must create professional situations and work environments that honor and respect what truly motivates their employees.

For example, Gregg Slager, senior partner for Ernst & Young, was known to work 80-hour weeks to complete billion-dollar deals for his clients and his organization. He made a lot of money, but at what cost? *FORTUNE* Magazine details that, "… at age 45, with 4 and 6 year old boys at home, he often found himself wondering whether the sacrifices were worth it. Vacations had become merely a

© 1998 Ted Goff

"There! Isn't that motivational?"

change of work venue. Some nights his wife, Sue, would bring the kids to his office in their pajamas so that they could spend some quality romping-around time with their dad. Something had to give."

The awareness and wisdom light bulb went off in Slager's mind when he realized he was missing precious time with his children. He was also losing great talent within the organization, and he was in the final stages of chronic workplace burnout. From that moment, he assertively and proactively began to change his work environment to increase loyalty and sustain motivation from his colleagues and employees. As a senior partner, he listened to his colleagues and employees to discover what motivated them the most: having a personal life outside of the office. *FORTUNE* Magazine reported, "So this year Slager did something taboo for a top performer in a world-class firm; he declared this wasn't the kind of life he and his team wanted." By reaching out and communicating with colleagues and employees, this senior partner changed the entire way his organization operated. Every job description was re-evaluated, and tasks were reallocated. As a result, the team ended up with better personal and professional lives and the quality of service the team provided to clients increased. "Weekend work is no longer the norm. And a manager who works for Slager says his family has stopped threatening to throw away his BlackBerry" (*FORTUNE*).

When colleagues and employees become mentally, emotionally, and physically overwhelmed and overburdened with work, they tend to withdraw from their colleagues, their leaders, and the organization as a whole. Of course, every professional job has its busy seasons in which colleagues and employees are expected or required to dedicate more time and energy by arriving early and leaving late. However, relationship-based leaders intentionally intervene before professional exhaustion and workplace burnout erodes the spirit of the organization's greatest assets: its employees.

Progressive and proactive organizations understand that motivating colleagues and employees to accomplish organizational goals means helping each employee accomplish her or his own personal and professional goals, which almost always consists of more family and social time outside the workplace.

Colleagues/Employees Answer the Question:
"How Can a Leader Best Motivate Me?"

- Give me autonomy and the freedom to do my job; please don't micro-manage me.

- As Jerry Macguire says, "Show me the money ($$$)."

- Give me time off and a flexible work schedule.

- Give me a promotion.

- Praise and recognize me when I am doing great work.

- Have confidence in me and in my skills.

- Let me have the freedom to make mistakes without punishment.

- Let me ask questions without making me feel dumb or stupid.

- Provide internal and external incentives and/or benefits.

- Tell me the purpose of the project because I like to know what I am doing, and I like to see how everything ties together.

- Clearly communicate what you expect from me as an employee.

Inspirational Leadership

Inspiration is the ability to encourage, energize, excite, and stimulate colleagues and employees. Inspiration is the "fire" or the spark of energy a team member brings with her or him to school or work. The Latin root of the word "inspire" is to "breathe life into"; therefore, relationship-based leaders who lead with greatness must breathe life into their employees in order to inspire them. The employees of any organization must have energy in order to achieve and accomplish the organization's purpose, vision, and goals; leaders must assist colleagues and employees with the necessary encouragement, energy, enthusiasm, and drive to maintain and sustain motivation. The right amount of energy will provide colleagues and employees with the drive to stay on task until their goals are accomplished. Inspiration provides employees with hope, and when employees have hope, they believe that reaching their agreed-upon goals is possible. Believing that goals are possible and achievable matters when a person pursues her or his personal and professional dreams, goals, and aspirations, because colleagues and employees are more motivated when goals are within reach. No colleague or employee wants to work towards unattainable and unrealistic goals. Study the various grassroots movements in American history and you'll find whenever the followers lost hope and belief in the possibility of attaining their goals, the movement stopped. In contrast, when the followers maintained hope and believed attaining the goals were possible, they kept moving towards the goals, even in the most difficult times. Inspiring your colleagues and employees means helping them set attainable goals in areas that matter to them and, in turn, helping them achieve those goals.

College President as an Inspirational Leader

Dr. Larry Litecky, the president of Century College, the school at which I teach, recently inspired me. We were faced with difficult budget cuts, and I knew from past experience that staff training and faculty development funds were usually among the first items to be axed. Instead, Dr. Litecky surprised me by refusing to cut the funds

© 2005 Ted Goff

"I have some great new leadership
ideas I want you to find inspiring."

for faculty and staff development. That's when I realized he support-ed professional development and valued life-long learning. His actions showed that he respected my colleagues and I as professional educa-tors. He knew the best way to grow Century College as an institution was to invest in faculty and staff through continuous and ongoing education. Dr. Litecky's decision not to cut faculty and staff develop-ment funds breathed new life into me personally and professionally. I felt honored, valued, and inspired by his decision. I was inspired because I want to be the best communications professor I can be and having the opportunity to attend conferences and workshops enables me to grow and develop tremendously. This allows me the opportunity to meet other professionals within my field, build great networks, and learn best practices within my discipline. It helps me avoid becoming rusty as a professional or burnt out as an educator.

As a relationship-based leader, providing inspiration means that you need to know what matters most to your colleagues and employees and to make efforts to understand what is important to them could possibly be quite different from what matters most to you. It is important for you to provide inspiration to your team and to encourage this inspiration among team members as well. Leaders must understand and accept that colleagues and employees are inspired by their own values—not solely by the leader's values. All colleagues and employees are inspired in different ways. When leaders embrace this idea, they will find inspiring colleagues and employees much easier. Showering your team with inspirational words and actions or "sparks of energy" can last the length of the meeting, but encouraging them to shower each other with their own sparks of energy lasts an eternity.

Colleagues/Employees Answer the Question: "How Can a Leader Best Inspire Me?"

• Believe in me and my abilities to do my job.

• Give me credit for my work (don't steal my ideas).

- Allow me to fail and make mistakes without punishment.

- Remember to say and give a personal "thank you."

- Make-work fun, interesting, and exciting.

- Get the entire team involved every now and then to build team unity.

- Give me challenging and stimulating work so I don't get bored.

- Don't waste my talents; let me do what I'm good at.

- Respect the quality of my work, creative ideas, and suggestions.

- Allow me to be myself at work; don't force me to be like everyone else.

- Be enthusiastic as a manager or leader.

- Give me the necessary tools, equipment, and resources to do a great job.

Influential Leadership

Influence is the ability to have a positive affect on a person based on your attitude, behaviors, character, and respectful communication. Can a leader's attitude really affect the team's mood and morale? Absolutely! How a leader responds to workplace conflict determines how colleagues and employees classify a leader's attitudinal outlook. Is your attitudinal outlook usually optimistic or pessimistic? A leader's actions and behaviors definitely affect a team's mood and morale; consequently, what you do or don't do shapes your team's perceptions of your commitment to the team and the organization. Do you roll up your sleeves and get involved as a leader, or are you known as the "delegator"? Does your team see you as a servant leader? How do you communicate with your colleagues and employees? Are you abrupt, brash, or rude? Or are you cordial, kind, and respect-ful? How you talk with your colleagues and employees as a leader determines how they will respond to your questions and requests.

As a leader, you have the ability to influence people when you least expect it, and this ability begins with your attitude, behaviors, character, and communication approach. Influential leaders get things done and make things happen in the workplace by being the people who colleagues and employees want to imitate and support. Influential leaders tell the truth, even when the feedback is controversial, difficult, unpleasant, and unpopular. By engaging in honest and open communication, they avoid wasting their colleagues' and employees' valuable time and energy. Influential leaders consistently get voluntary commitment, involvement, and participation from their colleagues and employees. Influential leaders know they must earn and build trust by maintaining an optimistic attitude despite adversity and by displaying friendly behaviors and mannerisms despite visible frustration. Influential leaders know they *must* maintain an upstanding character when faced with ethical or moral dilemmas. They must practice emotional intelligence and model respectful communication during the most controversial and heated dialogues, discussions, and debates.

Influence occurs instantly and constantly, often just beneath our conscious minds. The influential leader affects and impacts her or his colleagues and employees without even knowing it at times. Influential leaders know they must

© 2002 Ted Goff

"Your boss says there's no hurry,
but can you have these ready
by tomorrow?"

create a healthy work environment that is fun, friendly, safe, and welcoming in order to influence their colleagues and employees positively.

How do you create this kind of environment as a leader? *One way is by complimenting the effort—noticing and acknowledging the efforts your team is currently putting forth.* Many leaders ONLY celebrate with their teams when the organization's goals have been reached, achieved, and accomplished. I call it leadership suicide when leaders fail to acknowledge, applaud, compliment, praise, and recognize the ongoing efforts of their colleagues and employees. Team members need, and must have, cheerleaders from start to finish. Relationship-based leaders are cheer-leading leaders as well. I discovered this when I taught fifth and sixth grade to homeless youth in downtown Minneapolis. I saw amazing results when I encouraged students throughout the entire project from beginning to end rather than right before they reached the end of a project or school assignment. I noticed the students felt acknowledged, cared for, and valued when I complimented their ongoing efforts and progress. I found that when I modeled "complimenting the effort" as a relationship-based teacher and leader, the students smiled more frequently and were more engaged. Then, I noticed that the students began to compliment the efforts of one another. This is a clear and vivid illustration of leading by example.

Complimenting the effort is a powerful tool leaders can employ to motivate, inspire, and influence teams to keep moving the organization forward, especially in the face of budget cuts and low team morale. If you consistently display a positive attitude, professional behavior, ethical character, and respectful communication, your colleagues and employees will see those traits as the standard to emulate in their own work life, and this kind of influence can continue for many years. The ability to influence team members ethically is a fundamental attribute you must cultivate and develop in order to lead an organization successfully.

Cheerleading and Complimenting the Effort—A True Story

In college, my good friend Teresa was an avid runner who participated in three to five marathons annually. I was always amazed at her ability to finish in record-breaking times. I asked, "Okay, Teresa, what's your secret?" She replied, "It's mental, physical, and social preparation." I understood the mental and physical preparation, the stamina and fortitude it takes to complete marathons, but I wasn't quite grasping the concept of "social preparation" as one of her secrets of success. She explained that she invited anywhere from eight to fifteen family members, friends, and coworkers to support her during the race but encouraged them to spread out at three-mile intervals. She asked them to make signs with her name on them in bright neon colors. As she passed her friends and family members, she asked them to yell out her name along with powerful and encouraging words and phrases to help her sustain motivation and determination for the duration of the marathon. A week after the race, she would make an extravagant dinner for everyone and thank them personally for their support. She would often say, "When I felt like giving up, I didn't because I knew I had cheerleaders every three miles, and that kept me going until I crossed the finish line." This is the essence of complimenting the effort. In order to succeed, colleagues and employees need encouragement regularly. I hope you use this powerful idea to move your organization forward. I promise you that your colleagues and employees will greatly appreciate this kind of acknowledgment, encouragement, and recognition for their many work-related efforts.

Complimenting the effort is an important practice, especially when the task at hand doesn't have an immediate end in sight. *Time* Magazine, for example, did an excellent job of complimenting the effort and helping to sustain motivation for Dr. David Ho and his team of AIDS researchers. In 1996, *Time* named AIDS researcher and pioneer Dr. David Ho, "*Time* Person of the Year," a prestigious title crediting a person, couple, group, idea, or machine that has influenced events in the preceding year. This was a powerful form of acknowledgment, recognition, and motivation for someone who hadn't yet discovered a known cure for AIDS; even now, in the new millennium, there is no known cure. *Time* showed they valued Dr. Ho's pursuit of a cure by acknowledging and recognizing the progress that Dr. David Ho and his research team were making even though they had not yet met their ultimate goal. The acknowledgement, recognition, and encouragement provided them with the motivation needed to keep pursuing their organization's purpose, vision, and goal: finding a cure for AIDS. While I've never met Dr. David Ho, I believe he must have felt elated, inspired, and motivated when he saw his face on the front cover of *Time* Magazine. How can you as a leader emulate the philosophy of *Time* Magazine to motivate, inspire, and influence your colleagues and employees to keep moving forward?

Colleagues/Employees Answer the Question: "How Can a Leader Best Influence Me?"

- Apologize/admit when you are wrong and/or have made a mistake.

- Let me disagree with you without being punished or being scared of losing my job.

- Match words and actions (Practice what you preach).

- Help my team and I complete our tasks (Get involved at times).

- Show that you really care about the people on the team.

- Be willing to do whatever you ask of the team.

- Be honest and transparent; don't be superficial, fake, or phony.

- Know what you are talking about, and don't b.s. people.

- Be confident and have real life experience, not theory.

- Don't gossip about others, and never play favorites.

- Listen to my concerns, needs, and issues.

Persuasive Leadership (A Gift and a Curse)

People often confuse influential leadership with persuasive leadership and even use the words interchangeably. I believe there is a distinct difference between the two, and I definitely favor influential leadership over persuasive leadership. Let me explain why. ***Persuasion is the process of winning a person over with emotions, facts, figures, and position power.*** Persuasion involves the use or misuse of a colleague's or employee's emotions, peppered with facts and figures, aimed at obtaining a particular response from that person. The very process of persuasion implies that an individual wants or needs to win an argument or a discussion to achieve their desired goals. A persuasive leader may win the argument because she or he has the best information accompanied by a compelling, captivating, and charming delivery. However, what does it really cost the persuasive leader who wins the argument or discussion, but wounds a colleague or employee in the process? It is important for leaders to remember that winning an argument can cost them their credibility and damage workplace trust and relationships if people feel disrespected, devalued, and dehumanized in the process. Some people automatically resist or shut down during the process of persuasion. They begin to develop feelings of irritation and resentment due to the pressure that often accompanies the process of persuasion. Relationship-based leaders cannot afford to have valuable colleagues and employees shut down emotionally because organizational goals may never be achieved once emotional shutdown occurs.

I once knew an English professor who seemed to embrace the idea of persuasive leadership. He used a great deal of aggression, intensity, and force in his tone, actions, and delivery, and often communicated with rigid body language during his presentations. While he might have gained their attention, he clearly scared and intimidated his students. Persuasion definitely has its place in exceptional situations, but its excessive use will not help anyone become a relationship-based leader. Because it can damage interpersonal interactions, persuasion is not a catalyst for building deliberate interpersonal relationships with colleagues and employees. Relationship-based leadership is the key to effectively motivating, inspiring, and influencing colleagues and employees.

I have a few personal sayings, which I refer to as Jermaine-isms (which you will continue to see throughout the book), including the following, *"Winning can equal losing, and losing can equal winning."* If you win an argument but lose your credibility and trust as a leader, the consequence is far more damaging in the long run than losing an argument and winning the respect of those you lead. Persuasion is a deliberate and forceful act, and the short-term result is rarely worth the long-term relationship effects. I recall leading a workshop at Disney World in Orlando, Florida. An enthusiastic young man from the University of Puerto Rico yelled

from the back of the conference center, "Jermaine, influential leadership is per-
manent and long-lived while persuasive leadership is temporary and short-lived."
I told him I absolutely agreed with his prognosis of influence and persuasion,
and, as a result, I jokingly invited him up on stage to finish the remaining forty-
five minutes of my presentation because he was so on target with his comment.

When persuasion does not work, leaders need to know the best strategies for leading through the three main components of leadership: motivating, inspiring, and
influencing colleagues and employees to achieve the organization's goals. Now, to
help you implement these three components of leadership, I am going to introduce a tool that I developed called the D.A.L.O. Approach. The D.A.L.O.
Approach is an interpersonal communication tool created to help leaders get to
know their colleagues and employees better. The D.A.L.O. Approach was
designed to help leaders learn and understand how to best motivate, inspire, and
influence each individual within their organization.

THE D.A.L.O. LEADERSHIP APPROACH

I am often asked, "Jermaine, how do I go about finding out what really motivates,
inspires, and influences each person on my team?" That's when I introduce the
D.A.L.O. Approach. Quite simply, it means employing the following human
relations and interpersonal communication skills before attempting to manage or
lead a team of people:

Dialogue – A dialogue is an honest and open conversation where
there is an exchange of diverse ideas and perspectives.

Asking Questions – The respectful process of gaining and gathering
significant information about colleagues and employees to enhance
and improve work relations.

Listen – The process of hearing, honoring, respecting, and understanding colleagues and employees without interruption.

Observe – The process of paying close attention to colleague's and
employee's personal and professional hobbies and interest.

This approach works for individuals and teams alike. Additional names for the D.A.L.O. Approach are "Leadership by Walking Around" or "Leadership by Interpersonal Interactions." Using the D.A.L.O. Approach doesn't involve micro-managing your colleagues and employees or checking up on them; instead, it assists you in building interpersonal relationships between your colleagues and employees. The D.A.L.O. Approach will help you improve your communication with your colleagues and employees by teaching you how to demonstrate that you care about them and that their work matters to you as their leader.

Dialogue and Discussion

The first step of the D.A.L.O. Approach is to establish a safe and comfortable environment where colleagues and employees are willing to engage in open and honest dialogue with you as their leader. *A true dialogue is a conversation where there is an exchange of diverse ideas and perspectives.* While taking the time to engage in a dialogue and discussion with your colleagues and employees, you have the opportunity to learn the most about their beliefs, expectations, needs, and values. Can your colleagues and employees tell you the truth even when it hurts? Relationship-based leaders cherish the moments when their team is engaged in open and honest dialogue not only with them individually but also with the entire team. Through this process, there is an opportunity to deepen the relationship by asking informational and specific questions to learn what really motivates, inspires, and influences team members.

Ask Questions

The second step of the D.A.L.O. Approach is asking questions. The process of asking questions helps you, as a relationship-based leader, to gather significant and pertinent information about your colleagues and employees. Asking questions will help you gain a deeper insight into their aspirations, career interests, and T.A.G.S. (Talents, Abilities, Gifts, and Skills). Some questions to ask your colleagues and employees that will help you begin your journey as a relationship-based leader include:

- What motivates you intrinsically?

- What motivates you extrinsically?

- What inspires you personally and professionally?

- How can a leader or colleague best influence you?

- How can a leader tell when they are asking too much of you professionally?

- Are there any types of projects that interest you more than others?

- How can a leader tell when you are burning out in the workplace?

- What hobbies and interests do you have outside of work?

- What can a leader do to de-motivate you?

- Where do you see yourself in the short-term and the long-term within this organization?

- How do you like to be rewarded or recognized?

Listening

There are many fatal flaws in leadership, but the one fatal flaw I hear over and over again is, "She doesn't listen to us" or "He doesn't listen to us." This is why listening is the third step of the D.A.L.O. Approach. Pride, stubbornness, and arrogance often interfere with great listening. Whether you believe that statement wholeheartedly or not, there is definitely some validity to it. The cover of the June 2002 issue of *FORTUNE* Magazine read, "Why Companies Fail – 10 Fatal Mistakes (And How to Avoid Them)." Reading about all ten fatal mistakes was extremely informative, and I believe every leader should make sure these mistakes don't happen within her or his organization. The one fatal mistake that we are going to focus on from the article is "Fearing the boss more than the competition." The anecdote from *FORTUNE* that illustrates this fatal leadership flaw of not listening reads as follows:

"... Samsung Chairman Lee Kun Hee in 1997 decided to take Samsung into the auto business. Knowing the car industry was a crowded field plagued by overcapacity, many of Samsung's top management silently opposed the $13 billion investment. But Lee was a forceful chairman and a car buff to boot. So when Samsung Motors folded just a year into production, forcing Lee to spend $2 billion of his own money to placate creditors, he expressed with surprise: How come nobody had spoken up about their reservations?"

Mr. Lee failed to create a safe and comfortable environment where his colleagues and employees could openly and honestly discuss their diverse ideas and perspectives. They were especially careful NOT to disagree with Mr. Lee for fear of career retaliation and other repercussions. They didn't believe he would really— and I mean *really*—listen to their ideas and perspectives with an open mind; therefore, they proceeded with fear and avoided talking with him whenever they could. As a relationship-based leader, you should realize that it pays to listen to your colleagues and employees; in fact, this should be an expectation prior to your attempt to lead your team towards the organization's goals. Imagine how great and empowered colleagues and employees would feel if a leader asked them their ideas and opinions sincerely and actually *listened* to their responses! How would people perceive you as this kind of leader? How much more credible and influential would you become as a leader? Henry David Thoreau knew a great deal about empowerment and the impact of listening when he said, "The greatest compliment that was ever paid me was when one asked me what I thought, and attended to my answer." A leader who listens can significantly boost the morale of a team and organization as a whole. I hope you are listening!

Observations

Lastly, the fourth step of the D.A.L.O. Approach involves making observations. This doesn't mean you should walk around prying, snooping, and micro-managing colleagues and employees, since these behaviors will surely annoy, irritate, and de-motivate colleagues and employees. They will believe and feel you don't trust them as professionals. Instead, observation means paying close attention to employees' surroundings—their cubicles, clothing, mannerisms, and interests.

This attentiveness and awareness will provide you with great insights into your colleagues' and employees' lives and will help you communicate better with and motivate your team. You aren't being intrusive, nosy, or critical; you're simply getting to know each person, what she or he likes, and what her or his hobbies and interests are. You want to create an environment that allows your colleagues and employees to bring their whole selves and authentic selves to work.

By following these four steps of the D.A.L.O. Approach, you will find motivating, inspiring, and influencing your colleagues and employees much easier to accomplish.

Real-World Challenge: Mark seems distracted on the job and misses several deadlines. You find out from a colleague that his wife has cancer and is going through chemotherapy. How would you, as Mark's leader, handle this situation?

PART TWO

The Importance of Credibility

Courageous and Cowardly Leadership

I remember my mother uttering the statement, "Stand up for what you believe in J.D., and don't allow people to take advantage of you." To this very day, those words resonate with me emotionally and are at the core of my very being. However, she never told me I would need courage to implement her sound advice. As a teenager, I quickly discovered that you maintain relationships and gain more friends when you follow the norm and agree with popular actions and ideas. This way of being and thinking never meshed well with my personality. As a result, I began to experience deep feelings of personal betrayal, discomfort, fear, and internal conflict because I did not have the courage to stand up for my beliefs. I wanted to be bold and courageous, but at the time, my fear was far greater than my courage to be myself. Whenever I didn't stand up for what I believed in, I felt as if I was dying internally, and I felt like a coward. I realized that seeking social acceptance and approval cost me my manhood and personal integrity. I now know the true meaning of Tupac Shakur's powerful line, "A coward dies a thousand deaths, a soldier dies but once." How much of yourself do you lose when you don't take a stand for your beliefs?

When I was younger, I wanted to desperately have it all—friends, popularity, social acceptance, and social approval—but I also wanted the ability to be myself and to disagree without losing friends. I rapidly learned that not following the expected norm could cost me relationships, popularity, social acceptance, and social approval within certain homogeneous communities. There were times when I stood my ground and followed my convictions, and there were times when I behaved cowardly, and betrayed my authentic self. Whenever I behaved in a cowardly manner, I felt a deep emptiness and void in my soul and spirit; I was overcome with internal guilt for not being true to myself and real with those around me. Now I understand why William Shakespeare wrote in *Hamlet*, "This above all: To thine own self be true." I believe individuals possess a special kind of dignity, pride, and respect when they are comfortable and courageous enough to be themselves and be truthful with themselves and others.

You may be asking yourself, "What's the relationship between credibility, cowardice, courage, and leadership?" A whole lot! All leaders, even horrible leaders, must confront and overcome adversities, barriers, challenges, obstacles, and uncertainties in order to move their organizations forward. However, some leaders refuse to face certain adversities, barriers, challenges, obstacles, and uncertainties because of fear or because of a lack of courage. If a leader is not courageous enough to face her or his fears and problems head on, she or he tends to handle leadership challenges and problems in one of three ways: (1) *avoid* the problem; (2) *deny* the problem; or (3) *minimize* the problem. Of course, avoiding, denying, and minimizing team or organizational problems will inhibit growth and, ultimately, destroy the leader's credibility. Avoidance, denial, and minimization are three deadly poisons (I'll cover poisons more in depth when we discuss conflict) that relationship-based leaders never want to spread throughout their organization.

Does a leader really need courage to lead with greatness? Absolutely! It is impossible to lead an organization successfully without courage. You may be asking yourself, "So what exactly is courage?" After careful thought, meditation, and research, my definition of *courage is the mental, emotional, and physical strength to face fear and problems head-on.* Leaders are always faced with challenges and problems; what makes the job difficult for some leaders is the avoidance, denial, or minimization of organizational challenges and problems. I want to be clear regarding courageous leadership. Courage doesn't mean you don't have fears. Of course you have fears! You make critical decisions that affect the entire organization and your colleagues' and employees' careers! However, a relationship-based leader doesn't allow fear to stop her or him from moving forward and making the best decisions for the team. Some leaders allow their fear of failing or making mistakes to debilitate them to the point where they constantly procrastinate and become completely indecisive. Such action affects the leaders' credibility because colleagues and employees lose faith, hope, and confidence in these leaders' ability to make tough decisions and, essentially, in their ability to lead effectively.

You are human, so it is perfectly normal to experience fear; however, it is *not* okay to allow fear to prevent you from *Leading with Greatness*. Mark Twain once said, "Courage is resistance to fear, mastery of fear, not absence of fear." In truth, fear is an emotion that can be both facilitative and debilitative for leaders. It is a total misconception that courageous leaders don't feel fear—great leaders feel the fear but muster up enough strength to face fear head-on. Great leaders don't submit to and obey their fear factors. Courage is crucial to relationship-based leadership because it provides the fuel relationship-based leaders need to be able to say, "No" when necessary, to terminate problem employees, to advocate for raises and promotions despite budgetary constraints, and to make tough, controversial, and/or unpopular decisions. Courage lives in the deliberate actions relationship-based leaders take to overcome personal and professional challenges. Courage allows us to face the dangers and risks in life, school, and work. I believe that's why Walt Disney said, "All our dreams can come true, if we have the courage to pursue them." Now ask yourself how a leader might stop the growth of her or his organization if she or he lacks courage?

The 1939 American movie classic, The *Wizard of Oz*, introduced to audiences one character that pursued courage because he couldn't be the individual he wanted to be without it. This character, the Cowardly Lion, meets Dorothy Gale as she embarks on a magical trip to the Emerald City to meet the Wizard of Oz, who supposedly has the power to grant any wish. The Lion wishes, more than anything, for courage. He lacks so much courage that, at the movie's start, he can barely walk straight or hold his head up. His speech was filled with hesitation and uncertainty, he was indecisive and fearful. I bring up the Cowardly Lion because, unfortunately, many leaders who are otherwise task competent and intelligent behave like the Cowardly Lion when confronted with difficult interpersonal conflicts. Leadership is easy when everyone agrees with you and everyone is on your side; the real test of a leader's credibility comes when chaos, conflict, and differences of opinion over critical issues arise. Before his untimely death, Dr. Martin Luther King, Jr. spoke to this very issue when he wrote, "The ultimate measure of a man is not where he stands in moments of comfort and convenience, but where he stands at times of challenge and controversy." Leaders must have the courage to tell the truth to their leaders, colleagues, employees, customers, boards of directors, and shareholders. Additionally, and perhaps most importantly, leaders must also have the courage to be honest with themselves. Relationship-based leaders cannot be Cowardly Lions who are afraid of workplace conflicts. Fortunately, courage is something that can be developed, and anyone can find it, just as the Lion did. Courage does not require a magic wish granted by some all-powerful wizard, and it certainly doesn't happen instantaneously. It must be practiced and cultivated over time, but it can be done. I once heard Lee Mun Wah, Chinese American filmmaker of the critically-acclaimed documentary, *The Color of Fear*, say about courageous individuals, "Being courageous does not mean that you are not scared. I think that courageous acts are those taken by ordinary scared folks who simply hang in there thirty seconds longer than the rest of us." When the Lion finally stands before the Wizard of Oz and asks for courage, he is told he already has it. At that point, he has already stood up for himself and for his beliefs to the Wicked Witch of the West.

Cowardly Lions in leadership positions lack the ability to motivate, inspire, and influence colleagues and employees to accomplish organizational goals. Colleagues and employees want to follow the courageous leaders' guidance. Semantically, the word "coward" can evoke negative emotions and perhaps defensive responses, but understanding cowardly leadership is an important variable in building credibility. *A cowardly leader is one who lacks the mental, emotional, and physical strength to deliberately face fears, challenges, and conflicts head-on.* She or he allows doubt, fear, negative internal dialogue, social approval, and uncertainty to overshadow her or his courage to succeed. Fear eventually undermines her or his ability to lead with greatness.

Moving from Cowardly Leadership to Courageous Leadership

1) Acknowledge and name your fear. Moving from cowardly leadership to courageous leadership begins with acknowledging and naming the fear that prevents you from taking effective action and from being the relationship-based leader you really want to be. Are you fearful of being fired for telling the truth? Are you fearful of being disliked? Are you afraid of hurting someone's feelings? What do you think would happen if you became who you really want to be as a leader? I once coached a leader who was afraid of firing a popular person in the organization who really deserved to be terminated. I asked him, "What's really preventing you from letting this person go when you and people within human resources have documentation to support your decision?" He replied, "I really have two fears, Jermaine, I am afraid of what people will think of me and how they will respond to me, and I feel bad about firing someone who has a family, a mortgage, and bills to pay." Many leaders find themselves in similar predicaments. Acknowledging, naming, and addressing your fears with a plan for overcoming them is the first step in moving from cowardly leadership to courageous leadership. When the leader in this story acknowledged and named his fears truthfully, he developed mental, emotional, and practical strategies for dealing with his anxieties, concerns, and fears.

2) Find out what information you need to acquire in order to overcome your fears. Ralph Waldo Emerson says it best, "Knowledge is the antidote to fear." Typically, people fear what they don't understand. When leaders, colleagues, and employees lack the know-how to overcome their fears, they tend to procrastinate. If people perceive their personal or professional problems as too complex or too overwhelming, they will probably avoid their problems. The best way to overcome fear is to discover what information and resources you need in order to reduce or eliminate your fear entirely. In the previous story, the leader wanted to know how to respond to potentially irate and disgruntled colleagues and employees in the event of a popular coworker's firing. He was fearful because he lacked the mental, emotional, and practical know-how for dealing with the matter. While he did not eliminate his fear completely after learning what to do and how to respond, he was able to attend to the situation with more confidence once he had adequate information and resources.

3) Seek help and support, if necessary. We can all use a helping hand from time to time. Never be too afraid or too proud to use or leverage your colleagues' and employees' expertise and experience. When you feel afraid or don't know how to proceed, send an e-mail, pick up the telephone, or walk over to a colleague's or employee's desk or office and yell, "Heeeeellllllllllppppp!" A former colleague of mine, Gerry Perrin, had taught communication classes at Century College for over thirty years and was on the brink of retirement. She had one semester (sixteen weeks) left of her college teaching career. It was my first year as a professor at Century College, and one afternoon she knocked on my office door. She said, "Can I bother you for a minute? I'm struggling with classroom participation in a couple of my classes this semester. Do you have any ideas on how to get students more involved in classroom discussions?" Bewildered and dumfounded, I thought, "This woman has taught college longer than I've been on mother Earth, and she's seeking *my* one-semester-rookie advice?" Perrin retired one semester later, but she left me with a clear understanding of the importance of humility, no matter the rank, position, or years of experience. Why? We can all use assistance when uncertainty, fear, and ignorance interfere with personal and professional growth. Asking for help is a key strategy for overcoming fear and *Leading with Greatness*.

Confronting your challenges, fears, and problems happens on a weekly, if not daily, basis as a leader. It's essential that someone who wants to lead with greatness makes these confrontations positive and deliberate actions. The more you practice this, as a relationship-based leader, the more your confidence increases and the sooner you move from being a cowardly leader to becoming a courageous leader.

THE 5 C'S OF BUILDING CREDIBILITY AS A LEADER

A leader who has no credibility with colleagues and employees is not a leader at all, regardless of her or his position, title, skills, or connections with the organization's movers and shakers. If you are going to become a relationship-based leader, you first need to be a *believable* leader. A leader's credibility resides in her or his believability. People follow leaders they respect, trust, and believe in. Credibility is the vehicle leaders use to sustain trust over a long period of time. Team members easily follow leaders they trust. Try leading a team of people when they don't trust, respect, or believe in you, and I guarantee they will sabotage your leadership efforts. Leaders must establish credibility before they attempt to lead any team or organization. Credibility comes before trust in relationship-based leadership. When you use the 5 C's of building credibility, your status as a leader will increase exponentially and immediately.

1) Character: being authentic, sincere, and honest while showing integrity in all you do and say.

The Greek etymology of "character" means "to engrave and inscribe," which means to leave an imprint on a surface by carving, cutting, etching, printing, or writing. Leaders *always* engrave and inscribe their identities in decision-making situations. They are always under the organizational microscope, so they *must* be aware of *what* they engrave and inscribe. Your personal qualities and traits will distinguish you from others. A leader's character reveals her or his core values, ethical standards, guiding principles, and moral qualities. Being authentic is living in harmony with the personal and professional "stamp and imprint" you leave on those you lead. Character-based leadership implies that you are transparent as a leader: you don't hide the real you when you lead; it means you have *integrity*. You are an open book, read and analyzed by everyone in your organization. In *The Servant Leader*, James Autry addresses authenticity, "What does being authentic mean? Simply stated, it means be who you are. Be the same person in every circumstance. Hold to the same values in whatever role you have. Always be your real self." When colleagues and employees suspect a leader is fake or phony, they have difficulty following that leader. Organizational gossip and schisms might follow, and ultimately erode the organization's purpose, vision, and goals.

© 2002 Ted Goff

"I just found a place on the Internet where I can download all your work for free. You're fired."

On the other hand, when you are authentic and live congruently with your message, you demonstrate real character, and your colleagues and employees can recognize it and feel it. You deliberately choose to be truthful and honest with yourself and with those around you. Simply put, leaders *must* tell the truth. My grandmother always told me that every time you tell a lie, you have to keep dressing up the lie. "The more you lie," she said, "the more you have to embellish the lie to keep it believable." She would laugh and say, "Jermaine, lying is hard work, and it requires too much time and energy to keep up with all the details and specifics." In her age of wisdom, she would also remind me that she couldn't recall all the details and specifics even if she had wanted to tell a lie. She would say, "Always tell the truth, even if it hurts, because you will sleep better at night and people will respect you in the long run." Through my many experiences over the years and from the encouragement of my grandmother's words of wisdom, I've learned that it is utterly important for leaders to simply tell the truth.

I believe the root cause of all lies is fear—that's why I continue to stress the importance of courage. Sometimes leaders cannot muster enough courage to tell the truth, especially when the news is unfavorable, unpopular, or unpleasant. Some leaders choose to tell enormous lies; others tell white lies, half-truths or evade direct questions. They procrastinate, communicate indirectly, or become invisible, evasive, or ambiguous. These actions and inactions destroy a leader's character and, in turn, their credibility. In *Looking Out, Looking In*, authors Adler, Proctor, and Towne state, "75.8% of lies told were for the benefit of the liar. Less than 22% were for the benefit of the person hearing the lie, whereas a mere 2.5% were intended to aid a third party." While these statistics reveal that the majority of lies told are to benefit the liar, even telling lies to spare others' feelings will affect your image and credibility negatively once the truth finally emerges. While trust is earned over time, just one lie can instantly kill all you've strived to attain. As a leader, your credibility is earned one positive interaction at a time. The pressure is on; you must rise to the occasion. While you might see your character or integrity as a private or personal matter, it shines through in every interaction and team meeting. *Integrity can be defined as doing the right thing when no one else is looking; it is doing the right thing in all situations.* It's your integrity—and, therefore, your character—that helps shape your interpersonal experiences and also shapes the *communication climate—the emotional tone of the organization or relationships you have with your colleagues and employees.* While everyone in the organization is responsible for creating a positive and healthy work environment, those who lead with greatness model this perspective. They model what the environment should be like. In the workplace, character is the professional soul with which you make all your decisions, whether public or private. Ask yourself, "What is my character communicating on a daily basis to my customers, colleagues, and employees?"

2) Competence: having sufficient knowledge, T.A.G.S., and resources to do the job.

Competence is the second "C" of building credibility as a leader. Can you take your organization to the next level with your current T.A.G.S. (Talents, Abilities, Gifts, and Skills)? Do your colleagues and employees view you as professionally current and relevant as a leader? A competent person is ready, willing, and *able* to do the task at hand when she or he is asked to do so. When you first step into your leadership role, you want to be sure you're well prepared for the task. If you are provided with a written job description, follow it carefully and match your skills against it. If not, do your best to find out the expectations of your role before you begin to lead the team. You want to remember, too, that first impressions are vital. If you're fumbling professionally and lack the knowledge and resources needed to lead the team, your credibility will suffer as a result. Overly critical and cynical colleagues and employees tend to exploit leaders' incompetence by engaging in workplace gossip when they perceive the leader as incompetent. The ability to *listen* and *learn*, for instance, is crucial for developing leadership competence.

> ### *Your Employees Are Watching and Talking – So Listen!*
>
> When I speak at conferences, I can't believe how many employees complain about incompetent leaders, managers, and supervisors within their organizations. They complain about being fed up with people who occupy coveted leadership positions and yet lack the ability and skills to lead successfully. When team members feel their leaders are inadequate,

"You're such a great listener!"

they lack confidence in these leaders, which makes it extremely difficult to listen and follow their lead. I've seen organizations and/or departments become filled with envy, gossip, strife, and resentment as a result of incompetent leadership. This is why it is so important that you, as a relationship-based leader, put in the necessary time early on to learn the job. At a minimum you should build an effective team around you by hiring competent, smart, and savvy individuals who can compensate for your professional deficiencies and limitations.

Now, I would like to explore a few significant moments in U.S. history and to examine how these moments pertain to relationship-based leadership. All movements originate from a desire and/or need for change and are spearheaded by one individual or a small group of people. A leader is the catalyst for the movement, and the leader has the greatest impact on the direction, success, and sustainability of the movement she or he leads. People buy into the leader *first* and into the movement *second*; and leaders have the power to make or break those movements. In most cases in our history, it took the competence, charisma, drive, and leadership of a specific person to motivate people to follow them.

Here are some examples of competent leaders of movements and their visions:

Competent Leaders	Their Movements
Eleanor Roosevelt	Race, Poverty, and Women's Issues
Gandhi	Human Rights/Freedom from British Rule
William Lloyd Garrison	The Abolitionist Movement
Harriet Tubman	The Underground Railroad
Martin Luther King, Jr.	Civil and Human Rights Movement
Mother Teresa	The Poor People's Campaign
Socrates	Exploring Life through Asking Questions
Susan B. Anthony	Women's Suffrage Movement
Jimmy Carter	Volunteerism (Habitat for Humanity)
Joan of Arc	Liberation from British Occupation
Rosa Parks	Mother of the Civil Rights Movement

People Follow Competent Leaders and Their Vision

What I am trying to demonstrate with this example is that great leaders galvanize movements. People believe in and follow a leader before buying into a movement; therefore, in order for a movement to succeed, its leader must be competent.

People follow leaders for three compelling reasons:

Reason #1: The leader and the followers share a common interest.
Reason #2: The leader can relate to the experiences of her or his followers.
Reason #3: The followers trust their leader's T.A.G.S. to get the job done.

I would like to focus on Reason #3: Your employees and colleagues must trust in your ability as a leader to get the job done. In other words, no matter the cause, movement, or organization, followers want the personal satisfaction of working in an organization that is run by a leader who possesses the T.A.G.S. (Talents, Abilities, Gifts, and Skills) to achieve and accomplish the organization's goals. Take a moment to review the competent leader list, and explore what you think their T.A.G.S. were and how those T.A.G.S. related to the movements they led and represented.

Your colleagues' and employees' confidence and motivation increases when organizations and their leaders consistently succeed, win, and celebrate their teams' and organizations' victories. The confidence and motivation decreases when a leader's T.A.G.S. cannot support and drive the organization to the next level of success. This is why many athletic coaches are fired each year at the end of the season; followers will judge and measure a leader's competency level by what she or he achieves, accomplishes, and gets done. Would you continuously follow a leader who had little or no successes, wins, or victories? Probably not! How long would you follow a leader whose T.A.G.S. did allow her or him to continuously experience successes, wins, and victories? Let me know your thoughts on this when you see me next! Seriously!

3) Commitment: being devoted and dedicated to your team and the organization's purpose, vision, and goals.

What does commitment really mean? *A commitment is a personal pledge to follow through on an agreement or promise until completion or fulfillment.* Workplace commitment begins with a personal and professional pledge to always do your best to ensure team success. How can you tell if a leader, colleague, or employee is committed to the team or the organization? Can you tell by their words, intentions, or actions? I say you can always tell by their actions and the results they generate! Colleagues and employees determine and measure a leader's commitment by calculating her or his successes and results. They monitor your past and present achievements. Colleagues' and employees' opinions are formed by watching and monitoring a leader's contributions and by measuring her or his final results. Top management philosopher, Dr. Peter F. Drucker says, "The responsible worker (leader) has a personal commitment to getting results." I agree with Dr. Drucker; we can only measure the tangible and quantifiable results of a leader's commitment through observing what she or he has sacrificed personally and professionally for the company. It is through results that leaders can quickly quiet workplace critics, cynics, and whiners. *Your colleagues and employees cannot measure your intentions, but they can measure your actions.* Words and intentions do not matter to colleagues and employees if your actions don't follow. People want to know how much time and energy their leader is willing to give personally and professionally to ensure team and organizational success. Colleagues and employees want leaders to add value to the team and organization.

Famed Notre Dame Football Coach, Vince Lombardi once said, "Individual commitment to a group effort—that is what makes a team work, a company work, a society work, a civilization work." Within organizations, every team member brings her or his own level of devotion and dedication. Your role as a relationship-based leader means that you must convey the highest level of these attributes to your team. If you don't demonstrate belief in what your team is doing, no one else can be expected to show it for you. As a relationship-based leader, you demonstrate your commitment and build credibility through modeling the behaviors you want to see in your team and by working to achieve your goals. For some relationship-based leaders, such demonstration might mean arriving early and leaving late when necessary, volunteering for tasks, and showing that you, too, are willing to sacrifice in order to achieve team success.

The Committed CEO

I know a remarkable woman, Lynne Heidelbauer, who was the CEO of a small private hospital in Southern Minnesota. The typical nine-to-five office hours meant that most of the evening and night shift employees *never* saw her. She scheduled her work hours to include all shifts so that she could interact with evening and night shift employees. It wasn't unusual for her colleagues and employees to see her in the office at three a.m. Her sacrifice was plain for all to see. What did this schedule adjustment communicate to her colleagues and employees about her commitment to their success? Was Lynne's credibility increased or decreased as a result of her actions? Obviously, her credibility increased because her actions demonstrated her commitment. You, too, must show commitment to your employees if you plan to build credibility and lead with greatness.

4) Care/Concern: showing a high level of interest in the success of each individual person on the team.

I heard a quote many years ago, and I use it all the time when I teach the psychology of human performance and motivation. The quote simply states, "People don't care about how much you know—until they know about how much you care." If every leader kept this quote in mind when leading and communicating with employees, most organizational chaos and conflict would be reduced significantly. Colleagues and employees want to know whether their leaders really care about their personal and professional growth and upward mobility within the organization. Care and concern are the fourth vital "C" in the process of building credibility. If your colleagues and employees sense any degree of apathy from you regarding their professional development, career aspirations, or personal goals, they will begin to feel anxiety, fear, and resentment, all of which will interfere greatly with their ability to work creatively and innovatively. Yet, to stay competitive and to continue to produce superior and cutting edge products and services, you need colleagues and employees who are creatively and innovatively engaged in achieving organizational success.

The story of Mary Kay Ash is an example of how care and concern can contribute to the success of any organization. Mary Kay Ash took a $5,000 investment and turned her company, Mary Kay Cosmetics, into a billion-dollar corporation. She adhered to her mantra, "Make People Feel Important." According to her book, *More Than A Pink Cadillac*, "Mary Kay Ash used to advise her colleagues that they should think of every person around them—superior, subordinate, peer, field sales representative, mail carrier, whoever—as having a sign around her or his neck that said, 'Make Me Feel Important.'" When colleagues and employees feel appreciated, cared for, respected, and valued, there are three organizational benefits leaders can look forward to, says Ash:

1. Colleagues and employees will be more effective, efficient, and productive.

2. Colleagues and employees stay with the organization longer, reducing the attrition and turnover rate.

3. Colleagues and employees become more engaged, so the organization
   becomes more competitive as a whole.

Imagine I was your team leader, and after a brief team meeting, I distributed a
list of tasks for each team member to complete; also imagine that I did not
provide further direction or say another word about the tasks until our next
team meeting. First of all, I'm not complimenting everyone's efforts, but what
else does such an action say about my level of concern for our collective success? It demonstrates that if you lead with greatness, every aspect of achieving
the goal is important. This means that you stay involved and maintain a positive outlook throughout every step of the goal-setting and achievement process.
As a relationship-based leader, you gain excitement by seeing your colleagues
and employees succeed, and by assisting them in accomplishing their goals.
Your colleagues and employees want to know you care about them, their success, their work, and their career aspirations; they want you to believe their
ideas are important and worthwhile, or at minimum, worth considering.
Creating this environment for your colleagues and employees involves contin-
ual attention to each member of your team, as well as an understanding of her
or his role in achieving the team's goals. By demonstrating care and concern,
you will build and maintain credibility as a leader.

5) Charisma: the special qualities of an individual that draw people to them—the magnetic force that makes you favorable and like-able.

The Greek root of "charisma" means "to favor or divine favor"; in other words,
what makes you *"like-able"* as a leader? Ask yourself, "What special attributes,
characteristics, or qualities do I possess, which would compel colleagues and
employees to follow me?" When we think of charisma, we sometimes think of
someone who has a "big" personality—someone who is gregarious or eccentric.
We may think of people that can draw crowds and influence masses. In reality,
charisma can be considerably smaller than that. *Charisma means that you're
like-able and maintain a positive presence with and among your colleagues and
employees.* Charisma—your like-ability factor—can go a long way towards
building credibility. As a relationship-based leader, what is your *like-ability*
factor? What would you say naturally draws individuals to you personally and

professionally? A charismatic leader creates a fun and safe working environment by being friendly, humorous, sociable, and appropriately entertaining. You can demonstrate your charisma through simple actions such as smiling, possessing a friendly disposition, listening to others' experiences, conversing about non-work related issues, entertaining, and being intellectually competent and stimulating. Using the D.A.L.O. Approach to ask your colleagues and employees about their families, career interests, and hobbies outside of work allows your connection with them to go beyond standard workplace interactions. This behavior makes you appear more down to earth and approachable, and it reveals that you have an interest in the lives of others. Your charisma is what makes you a credible relationship-based leader—one that your colleagues and employees respect and enjoy working with.

Real-World Challenge: You are a college student selected as the leader of a team of classmates who must collectively write a marketing research paper for a class you are taking. You are a perfectionist when it comes to writing, and you are afraid your classmates will make errors that reflect on you. How can you prevent this from happening?

PART THREE

The Importance of Trust

Building Trust as a Relationship-Based Leader

It was a sunny Sunday afternoon in August 2000, when I conducted my first formal study on trust and its connection to relationship-based leadership. While I was lying on the floor in my office looking up the denotative definition of trust in my Merriam-Webster's Collegiate Dictionary, I had a significant revelation. *The Scandinavian root of the word trust implies feelings of comfort and demonstrations of confidence.* After I learned the word's root meaning, building, creating, and earning trust wasn't as abstract as many people had made it out to be. Don't get me wrong: I know that as human beings we are complex creatures. My revelation, however, revealed a less complicated approach to building trust and connecting with others. I learned quickly that relationship-based leaders can do a few practical things to begin the process of building, creating, and earning colleagues' and employees' trust.

Colleagues and employees need to feel safe and secure with their leader; they also need to believe and see certain behaviors in their leaders before they give her or him their trust. This is why it is so important for leaders to establish and build deliberate interpersonal relationships with their colleagues and employees before attempting to lead them. *Trust is created one interaction at a time.*

The old saying that "trust goes both ways" is true in the language of teams and in the experience of leading them. The only difference is that, in the world of leadership, the leader carries the greater load when it becomes reality. Ask yourself whether you are building and creating a trusting environment as a leader. The picture I see of a trusting environment is one of a comfortable setting where team members can feel at ease and safe within a friendly, open, inclusive, and welcoming work environment. It sounds idealistic, but if you understand that such a state cannot be achieved overnight, working toward that goal becomes achievable. Sometimes trust needs to be tested and strengthened through adversity, conflict, and differences of opinion. Trust truly does go both ways. As a relationship-based leader, you need to show that you carry a strong belief in the T.A.G.S. of your colleagues and employees. They must know that you see them as competent, dependable, and reliable. Your employees must know you believe in their abilities to get things done. Colleagues and employees must believe their leader is dependable in order to ultimately build trust. A leader's follow-through is extremely crucial to building team trust, and colleagues and employees will study a leader's track record to determine whether she or he is trustworthy. As the Russian proverb says, "Trust, but verify."

WHAT IS TRUST, EXACTLY?

In a personal, professional, or intimate relationship, trust is the combination of both comfort and confidence. I have developed an equation to illustrate how comfort and confidence are dependent on one another to build, create, and earn trust:

$$\text{Comfort} + \text{Confidence} = \text{Trust}$$

Comfort: to feel at ease and safe within a friendly and welcoming environment.

Confidence: having the full assurance or a strong belief in the reliability of a person.

© 1999 Ted Goff

OUR
PARANOID
FOUNDER

In the equations below, a leader cannot build, create, or earn trust without both variables being present:

$$Comfort - Confidence = Mistrust$$
$$Confidence - Comfort = Mistrust$$

Let me illustrate what happens when leaders separate comfort and confidence. Colleagues and employees can feel comfortable with a particular leader and have no confidence in her or him. Colleagues and employees could also, however, have a lot of confidence in a particular leader but not feel comfortable around that person. The following scenarios illustrate the effects of comfort without confidence and confidence without comfort.

Scenario A – Comfort without Confidence

The colleagues and employees of Shoestring Budget Advertising Agency, Inc. absolutely adore their leader, Elsa, and feel comfortable around her because she is always smiling, socializing, listening well, and celebrating team efforts. She is an absolute blast to work with; however, Elsa rarely gets things done. She is unorganized and misplaces important documents regularly. Her follow-through on tasks is equally as horrible. She is a fun person to be around, but her colleagues and employees can't depend or rely on her, her colleagues and employees mistrust her. Elsa's colleagues and employees lack confidence in her ability to accomplish the team and organizational goals. Elsa is incompetent when it comes to getting things done.

Scenario B – Confidence without Comfort

The colleagues and employees of Wrinkle Free Cleaners all agree that their leader, Keith, is competent, dependable, and reliable. They have confidence in Keith because he knows how to operate and fix the equipment when it breaks down. He is fast, accurate, and efficient; Wrinkle Free Cleaners rarely falls behind schedule when he is on duty. Since he's become store manager, Wrinkle Free Cleaners has earned and demonstrated a consistent profit, and as a result, the employees have all received their end-of-the-year bonuses. However, the employees absolutely despise working with Keith because he is a task-driven leader and views the workplace as exclusively for work at the expense of fun and relationships. People complain that he rarely smiles; he's uptight and impersonal. Although Keith does an exceptional job as a task-driven leader, he fails to create and reinforce a friendly, welcoming, and trusting working environment and culture at Wrinkle Free Cleaners.

PRACTICAL IDEAS FOR BUILDING, CREATING, AND EARNING TRUST AS A LEADER

The following suggestions for building, creating, and earning trust were taken from workshops and seminars I've conducted across the country since 2000. I always encourage both new and seasoned leaders to implement three to five suggestions at a time to begin the process of creating a culture and climate of organizational trust. As you review the following tables, ask yourself, as a relationship-based leader, how can you use these tips to begin the process of building trust within your team and organization.

These ideas have been tested and tried by leaders around the globe, and many leaders have regularly expressed through emails, letters, and phone calls how—once implemented—these ideas contributed to the success of their teams and organizations. It is my desire to help leaders and organizations create a high-trust culture for their colleagues and employees to thrive in through applying some of the ideas outlined in the illustrated tables.

Ideas for Creating COMFORT

- Smile often.

- Be empathetic (show you really do care about colleagues and employees).

- Be friendly and hospitable.

- Be outgoing.

- Be fun, and make work fun.

- Be interested in others.

- Be yourself (don't be phony).

- Involve others.

- Listen to others' ideas and opinions.

- Recognize, compliment, encourage, and praise others.

- Celebrate the team's accomplishments and achievements.

- Remember names.

- Have friendly and open body language (don't be stuffy and uptight).

- Show respect to others.

- Meet the team's basic needs.

- Be open-minded.

- Show optimism (especially during times of challenge, change, fear, and uncertainty).

- Give respectful eye contact.

- Make others feel like they are a part of the team.

- Allow people to bring their diversity to the team and organization.

- Consistently champion and cheerlead for the team.

- Advocate for what is right.

Ideas for Building and Demonstrating CONFIDENCE

- Be confident in yourself.
- Be truthful and honest.
- Be productive.
- Follow through on your word and tasks.
- Be prepared and ready.
- Communicate appropriately given the cultural context.
- Know your "stuff" and be knowledgeable.
- Acknowledge, admit, and apologize when you are wrong.
- Be open and transparent.
- Be motivated.
- Be a visionary leader.
- Adhere to ethical principles and responsibilities.
- Listen with empathy and without interruption.
- Be consistent.
- Set people up to succeed.
- Play people to their strengths and their T.A.G.S.
- Set the example by showing what confidence looks like.
- Acknowledge accomplishments, and don't steal other's ideas.
- Be fair.
- Be available.
- Consistently reach team goals.
- Periodically come in early, and leave late.
- Confront gossip.
- Deal with conflict immediately.

The following list of Jermaine-isms about trust is based on my personal and professional experiences as a teacher, speaker, facilitator, coach, and entrepreneur. I would like to make it clear that these ideas and thoughts are personal opinions that I believe can help you build trust with colleagues and employees on your journey and exploration to becoming a relationship-based leader.

13 Jermaine-isms of Trust that Every Relationship-Based Leader Should Know

1) You cannot rush the trust process.

2) People follow leaders they trust.

3) Credibility comes before trust in ALL relationships.

4) You must be trustworthy before you can earn people's trust.

5) It takes courage to trust others.

6) Trust is earned one interaction at a time.

7) Trust is the foundation of *all* relationships.

8) Where there is a lack of trust, doubt and suspicion are present.

9) Trust is the emotional and invisible glue that holds *all* relationships together.

10) Communication is effective, honest, and open when trust is present.

11) Once trust is lost, you *might* be able to regain it.

12) Once trust is lost, you may *never* be able to regain it.

13) Trust is powerful and precious—don't abuse it or misuse it.

REGAINING TRUST AS A LEADER WHEN TRUST IS LOST

The 18th century essayist and poet Alexander Pope wrote, "To err is human; to forgive is divine." Mr. Pope was keenly aware of fallible human nature when he wrote this simple yet profound and thought-provoking statement.

As fallible people, we sometimes anger, disrespect, hurt, offend, or irritate our close team members intentionally and unintentionally. This is more likely to occur during times of organizational change, chaos, conflict, and stress. Our fallibility manifests when leaders allow their arrogance, ego, pride, and selfishness to interfere with the good and successful direction of the organization. In *The 17 Indisputable Laws of Teamwork*, John C. Maxwell writes, "The goal is more important than the role." He argues that all successful organizations commit and adhere to the organization's purpose, vision, and goals, and that such commitment is more relevant and significant than the fancy positions and titles some leaders hold sacred. Some leaders, blinded with arrogance by their position and power, may begin—if not careful—to abuse and misuse that power. Some leaders destroy and burn personal and professional bridges in the workplace by damaging relationships through arrogance, ego, and bad attitude. This happens when leaders lose sight of the big picture and the organization's best interest or by putting their personal agendas ahead of team and organizational goals. Leaders are more likely to offend others, lose credibility, and destroy team trust when they lose sight of the organization's purpose, vision, and goals. Maxwell articulates that idea eloquently when he states, "If you think you are the entire picture, you will never see the big picture."

Hubris: Dangerous and Destructive Leadership

In ancient Greek tragedy and art, the major downfall of many leaders and heroes was their hubris. *Hubris is the excessive pride of a human being—the belief that one is far superior to peers (and even superiors).* Some of the best-known characters in Greek mythologies and tragedies—Odysseus/Ulysses, Achilles, Agamemnon, Lucifer, and MacBeth—destroyed their own lives and the lives of everyone who followed them because of hubris. They were too proud to take advice, listen to others' perspectives, or admit mistakes (much less apologize for their mistakes). People still suffer from hubris today. Leaders who are too proud or too arrogant to listen to their colleagues or employees can destroy and damage any work environment. Hubris-based leaders can create chaos and/or war, like MacBeth, or lose the loyalty of their team, such as when Odysseus' soldiers turned against him. Furthermore, an arrogant leader is more likely to make bad decisions that will affect the entire company because she or he does not take other viewpoints into consideration. To lead with greatness, one must have or demonstrate the opposite of hubris: humility. *Humility is the practice of managing and reducing one's arrogance and pride before it gets out of control.* A humble leader can build relationships with colleagues and employees by listening to her or his team's feedback, ideas, and advice. Humility is definitely a sign of emotional maturity.

Of course, even well-meaning leaders make mistakes. A loss of trust is like a physical blow that causes you to say, "Ouch!" It can cripple the team's progress if not attended to appropriately and promptly. For example, suppose you forgot everything you know about leadership and promoted a good friend without utilizing acceptable recruiting, hiring, and human resources channels. Even though your friend might have been the best person for the job and might have encompassed all the criteria to fulfill the position, your approach to the promotion more than likely hurt your colleagues and employees. This is a time when you need to become a healer and a leader by taking steps to regain your employees' trust in your leadership ability. To assist you with the process, I have outlined the 5 steps toward regaining trust as a leader in the section below.

The 5 Steps to Regaining Trust as a Leader

1. Acknowledge and admit what you did wrong.

To regain trust, it is imperative that you quickly acknowledge that you have offended a colleague or employee. This action takes an act of self-reflection, or what I call intrapersonal awareness, and it takes courage to own up to offensive behavior. *Acknowledgment means that you recognize that you have wounded a colleague or employee emotionally, personally, or professionally and that you are aware of how your actions or inactions have destroyed team trust.* The offense must register on your radar screen for you to be able to correct it. Due to hubris, some leaders find it difficult to acknowledge the fact that their behaviors foster organizational chaos, conflict, controversy, and gossip. Those who lead with greatness own the problems they've created, and take responsibility for correcting problems.

Once you are fully aware of how you've betrayed an employee's or team's trust, you must make an individual, team, or public announcement admitting that what you did was wrong, unacceptable, or unethical. Doing so is utterly necessary to regain trust. *Admitting is taking personal and professional accountability and ownership for your offenses by verbally confessing your unacceptable behaviors to those you have offended.* When leaders verbally admit to their mistakes and apologize sincerely, they are perceived as humble. But when a leader filled with hubris avoids admitting a mistake, she or he is perceived as arrogant, rude, self-righteous, and stubborn. What do you do as a leader when you have wronged your team or a member of your team? How do you go about correcting your offense?

2) Apologize: Ask for forgiveness, and negotiate how to proceed forward with the relationship.

As children, our parents told us to say, "I'm sorry" when we hurt someone's feelings, so we did, especially when our parents were standing there. However,

© 2004 Ted Goff

"It wasn't my fault. Someone put the wrong information in my notes, memos and letters to the customers."

my mother never explained to me the intricate details or the psychology of an apology. She taught me the standard process of apologizing. She'd say, "You apologize to others, Jermaine, when you've offended them because apologizing is the right thing to do." So, I did it because Mamma said so. If your parents or guardians were anything like my mother, you are probably not skilled in the art of apologizing, either. In my mother's most humble and sincere attempt, she failed to teach me how to apologize effectively. I learned to apologize effectively through dialogue, asking questions, reading books, and most of all, through trial and error. As a relationship-based leader, have you ever thought about how your apologies are perceived? Better yet, do you know how to apologize effectively?

An apology is a verbal and non-verbal expression of one's regret for hurting, offending, or wronging another person. However, most people don't know how to apologize effectively; they avoid the people they've hurt so that they don't have to acknowledge their mistakes or wrongdoings. Some hope and pray the situation will just disappear. Guess what? Problems never go away by themselves; problems need a leader's assistance for resolution. Problems only become worse when we avoid, deny, and minimize them. In one of the many books I've read, I came across a powerful quote that says, "What you resist only persists." Relationship-based leaders know that problems don't disappear magically on their own. Problems disappear when you confront them, deal with them, and work them out. There are some problems that leaders need to fix themselves, and there are others that certain departments or the entire organization must get involved in collectively.

Apologizing is having the courage to verbally and non-verbally own up to your mistakes and offenses. The longer a leader takes to apologize after committing an unethical, unthinkable, or offensive act, the more rapidly her or his credibility and influential power crumbles and diminishes. Time does matter when you've offended others and an apology delivered and offered in a timely manner is key to healing broken relationships. The longer people have to wait for their leader to apologize, the larger the divide grows between the leader and those who have been hurt. When leaders come around people they've offended and act as if nothing ever occurred, this is what their colleagues and employees think:

- My leader or colleague doesn't care about me.

- My leader or colleague is cooking up a juicy lie.

- My leader or colleague is so arrogant, egotistical, selfish, and stubborn.

- My leader is a bad leader and a coward for avoiding me.

- How did this idiot become our leader?

Hubris-based leaders often attempt to rectify the situation from their personal perspective. They rationalize or intellectualize the situation so they can feel better about the pain or frustration they've caused. Although their intentions are good, leaders gamble when they try to correct an offense from their own perspective rather than by incorporating the offended party's point of view. As a result, such leaders may not actually rectify the situation if their perspective is totally incompatible with the other's perspective. Rather, the leader must ask the offended person for advice on how to correct the wrong or mistake. This is the only way to re-establish trust. A leader may ask, "What would you like to see me change in my attitude and behaviors, or what would I need to do to help you trust me again? What is the best way for us to move forward as a team and organization?" Trust me on this piece of leadership advice. You will always be more effective in proceeding forward when you seek to incorporate the ideas and perspectives of the person(s) you've offended.

3) Behave your way out of the mess you have behaved your way into.

If you haven't already noticed, I love quotes! Poster quotes from family, friends, colleagues, students, and famous people decorate my office door and interior office. One quote in particular says, "There are no maids around here, and your mother doesn't live here—so you are responsible for cleaning up whatever mess you make around here." I purchased the poster at a dollar store when I first started teaching ten years ago because it reminded me of one of my mother's famous parenting phrases, "*You* make the mess, *you* clean the mess." It is leadership suicide when a leader refuses to apologize to wronged colleagues and employees. When leaders make professional messes in the workplace, they are responsible for cleaning up after themselves. Yes! Leaders have to clean up after themselves when they've betrayed and destroyed workplace trust. If leaders want to rebuild and regain the trust of their colleagues and employees, they must use their personal efforts and energies to fix any problems they've created. If leaders have others clean up their messes for them, they will be perceived as apathetic, cowardly, detached, hubris-filled, untouchable, and weak. It speaks volumes when leaders *don't* and *won't* clean up after themselves. On the flip side, it speaks volumes when leaders *will* and *do* clean up after themselves. As a leader, will you choose to take responsibility for your messes? Please choose wisely!

I attended a day-long leadership summit on June 15, 2005, in downtown St. Paul, Minnesota. I was excited about this leadership event because I could spend an entire day learning about leadership development and personal effectiveness from Rudy Guliani, former New York City mayor; Jack Welch, former CEO and Chairman of General Electric; and Dr. Stephen R. Covey, one of my all time favorite writers and teachers. When Dr. Covey entered the stage and embraced us with his presence, I was all ears, eyes, heart, and mind because I knew he was about to give me a few personal and career golden nuggets. Forty-five minutes into his presentation, I heard a statement that changed my life, "You cannot talk your way out of a mess you behaved your way into." I bit my bottom lip, clenched my pen, and said to my friend and virtual assistant, Jenny, "Did you hear what he just said? That was so deep." I don't believe the statement struck the same chord in Jenny as it did in me, but Covey's sentiment changed the way I do things. Too often in my personal and professional life, I have tried to talk my way out of messes that I have created by my own actions and behaviors. Now, of course, I realize I was operating incorrectly and inappropriately.

Most Americans are told early in life that actions speak louder than words. People don't and won't believe your words if they are not matched by appropriate actions and authentic behaviors. When leaders clean up their messes after creating a workplace mess, they must have a combination of words (a formal apology) and actions to prove they are sorry and serious about correcting their mistakes. Changing your actions and behaviors is the only way to show people you've changed. Your words won't matter if your actions and behaviors haven't changed. *Incongruency is when words and actions are not in alignment with one another.* Words that don't match actions and behaviors will only confuse the people who live and work with you.

If you have hurt, offended, or wronged a person, the best way to communicate to them that you are sorry is by showing them you have replaced the problematic actions and behaviors with new ones. Colleagues and employees will not believe you until they see change in your actions and behaviors. Nothing more and nothing less! Only then can trust be rebuilt, regained, and re-established. Colleagues and employees will continue to monitor how you act around them and others to confirm that you have changed. Remember what Dr. Covey said "You cannot talk your way out of a mess you behaved your way into." I like to say, "You must behave your way out of the mess you behaved your way into." *Congruency is when words and actions are in alignment with one another.* When your actions and behaviors change, you will have begun the process of rebuilding, regaining, and re-establishing the trust that was originally lost.

A True Story of Lies, Broken Promises, and Betrayal

When I was in grade school, my stepfather would promise every week to take me to see the Chicago Bulls, Chicago Bears, Chicago Cubs, or Chicago White Sox. I would run to school and brag to my schoolmates about this awesome weekend I was about to have. Well, on Mondays, I didn't want to go to school because I was too embarrassed to admit that my so-called awesome weekend never occurred—and I mean NEVER occurred. My stepfather had a drinking and partying problem, and he allowed drinking and partying to interfere with his ability to follow through on his commitments. His choices hurt and wounded me because I really wanted to see my Chicago Bulls (and yes, I was a Chicago Bull's fan even before they had the global superstar athlete, Michael Jordan).

After drinking and partying on the weekends, my stepfather spent his Sundays nursing hangovers, which meant he was too exhausted, too lazy, and too sick to follow through on his promises. He would apologize religiously, give me money to try to over compensate for his broken promises, and make new commitments only to fail me time and time again. I stopped believing in him, and I would quickly disregard his new promises because I didn't trust him anymore. I didn't hate him, but there were times when I cried deeply because I was tired of being hurt, lied to, and let down. I didn't understand how he could let me down repeatedly. Although I tried not to, I took it personally. I often thought he didn't like me. When he apologized, he was trying to talk himself out of a mess he behaved himself into, but after a while, his empty apologies didn't matter or work anymore. That experience taught me that actions truly do speak louder than words. As relationship-based leaders, please monitor your actions and behaviors, and follow through on your commitments! Your actions and behaviors are your keys to breaking the locks of doubt, mistrust, and suspicion. Please, use your keys wisely on your journey toward *Leading with Greatness*.

4) Be consistent and practice consistency.

When you commit verbally and non-verbally to correcting your mistakes, you make a new promise to eliminate the actions and behaviors that caused the problem and pain in the first place. If behaviors don't change you won't restore trust as a leader. There must be a change in your behavior to begin the process of restoring trust. To rebuild trust, you must be fully dedicated and devoted to doing the right thing routinely and to doing things right. Yes, you will be under the organizational microscope, but this is your opportunity to demonstrate that you are truly sorry and that you've learned your lesson. This is your chance to re-invent yourself personally and professionally. You can now demonstrate your commitment to the promises you've made to your team and the entire organization through your new set of actions and behaviors.

You may become overwhelmed emotionally, physically, and mentally with the notion of believing you have to be perfect in *all* of your actions and behaviors because of your colleagues' and employees' high expectations. Well, you do have to be perfect in most ways. People want your actions, behaviors, and words to be consistent, because this is the only way they can verify whether you really mean what you say. Because we are human beings and we do make mistakes and fall short of perfection, here's an idea to implement when you can't deliver on a commitment or promise: you *must*, and I repeat, you *must* communicate, communicate, communicate, and communicate. It is imperative that you communicate immediately and urgently. If you don't, you will forfeit any strides you've made previously with your colleagues and employees. You have to communicate to keep people in the loop. You must communicate to relieve your team of any ambivalence, uncertainty, or suspicion. You must communicate out of respect for others. Over the years, I've learned that when there is a communication and dialogue gap, people tend to draw their own emotionally-based and irrationally-driven conclusions. As a relationship-based leader, you can't afford to have people within your organization making emotionally-driven or irrational decisions that will interfere with your ability to motivate, inspire, and influence colleagues and employees to accomplish organizational goals.

5) Befriend time and patience.

Some people believe that time heals all wounds. But, as optimistic as that sounds and as optimistic as I am, I don't believe that time heals *all* wounds. I believe wounds can be healed when people and leaders are deliberate, intentional, purposeful, and proactive about practicing the act of forgiveness. How long does it take for colleagues and employees to forgive? Forgiveness depends on three variables: (1) how quickly the leader acknowledges, admits, and apologizes for her or his offense(s); (2) how quickly the leader actually stops the painful and problematic actions and behaviors; and (3) how willing those who were offended are to forgive you and move forward. If you have wounded someone, please understand that there is no exact art or science to when you will be forgiven. Remember, you cannot rush the trust process because trust is earned one interaction at a time. The hard truth about regaining trust is that it's easier to lose trust than it is to regain it. Just remember that you must change your offensive actions and behaviors to get the process started, and once it has started, remember that consistency and communication are all you can use to redeem yourself. Never forget that actions speak louder than words, and that trust is regained by a combination of actions and words. Your actions and words must be aligned with one another. Colleagues and employees want the assurance that their leader's offensive actions or words will never be repeated again. I know this process can be challenging, difficult, and overwhelming, but if you persist in doing the right thing, you can rectify most personal or professional problems you may have caused. Good success on your journey of regaining trust!

A Final Word on Rebuilding and Regaining Trust

In the eyes, hearts, and minds of some colleagues and employees, some acts are unforgivable. Forgiveness is an action and a process, and some people choose to forgive and move forward while others hold grudges and move backwards. When I work with teams and organizations, I see both kinds of actions within organizations, and the latter cripples and stifles organizational growth and prosperity. It takes two (or more) people to make the forgiveness process work. Remember, as a leader, your actions daily, weekly, monthly, and annually make all the difference. Trust and credibility go hand-in-hand when it comes to creating relationship-based leadership. So, please act accordingly!

© 1996 Ted Goff

"Here's the problem. You have a grudge wedged in your information pipeline."

Real-World Challenge: Your team has been assigned a series of tasks related to a new advertising campaign. Before the first meeting, a friend asks you to let her or him assume one of the most desirable jobs the team will handle, and you agree. When you arrive at the meeting, others are clearly upset by your decision to assign the task to your friend. What do you say to your team regarding your decision?

PART 4

What Do Others Expect of You as a Leader?

What Do You Remember of Your Leaders?

Think back to the various leaders with whom you've worked. How did they run their meetings? How could you tell they were team leaders? How did they make you feel as a team member? Were they friendly and personable? Did they micro-manage the team? Did they leverage all the team members' T.A.G.S. (Talents, Abilities, Gifts, and Skills)? Did they yell and scream? Were they effective listeners and communicators? Did they play favorites? Did they use a hands-off approach to managing and leading? My guess is that you can think of at least a few leaders who led their teams effectively but did so in ways that were quite different from other leaders you have witnessed. Not all leaders are the same. Leaders bring to the organization their own methods, philosophies, communication styles, personalities, and expectations, all of which have a significant effect on how the team and organization functions. Let's explore how this works.

DIVERSE LEADERSHIP STYLES: WHICH TYPE OF LEADER AM I?

Autocratic Leadership

Autocratic leaders try to maintain strict control over the team by regulating policies, procedures, and behaviors. An autocratic leader is not a team player in nature or practice. They are agenda-and-task-driven leaders. The autocratic leader has an ongoing to-do list *and* actually checks off the tasks as they are accomplished and completed. Because they see themselves as task-oriented, they lead their teams accordingly, often by giving direct orders. They set specific goals for each employee and clearly state their expectations. Organizations operating under autocratic leaders are more productive, highly efficient, and particularly effective during crises and tight deadlines. Autocratic leaders tend to credit themselves for the company's success and believe they are entirely responsible and accountable for all it produces. The autocratic leader's dominant belief is that work should come first and play second (if at all).

Colleagues and employees can struggle with the autocratic leader's one-way communication style. One-way communication, such as mandating jobs and giving orders, is one of the quickest and surest ways to demean, disrespect, and devalue colleagues and employees. This mode of communication says, "I'm superior to you, so listen to what I have to say. You're inferior, and I really don't want or have to listen to what you have to say." Creative approaches, innovative ideas, and opposing opinions from team members are generally not welcomed or accepted by autocratic leaders.

Additionally, an autocratic leader often takes all the credit for the team's successes, and thereby significantly lowers the team's morale. In fact, one of the greatest leadership crimes that can be committed against a fellow colleague or employee is to secretly confiscate or boldly steal intellectual property (creative and innovative ideas). A workshop participant once shared with me how he worked on a project for four months; he described how proud and prepared he was to present his work to the executive team. However, his manager convinced the employee to allow him to present the information to the executive team instead.

"Tell everyone who's been following my example that they're fired."

Within minutes of the presentation, this gentleman's heart dropped to the floor because his leader *never* acknowledged and credited him, the person who originated the great ideas. The employee said, from that point on, this particular leader had lost all credibility. As you can see, fear and mistrust often dominate team dynamics under autocratic leadership, and turnover rates often increase under an autocratic style of leadership as well. Autocratic leaders are sometimes perceived as leaders who lead from a control, demand, fear, or intimidation paradigm.

A friend of mine, Marlene, worked as a chemical engineer in a paper factory. She noticed that after six months of working for an autocratic leader, her own creative energy started to lag, and her ability to innovate began to deteriorate drastically. Marlene's autocratic leader, Rudolph, had a fixed and inflexible plan as to where the corporation was going, and meetings revolved around assigning duties to various team members without employee and team participation. Many workers despised attending the weekly team meetings although only a few would say so. Marlene achieved her weekly work goals but only out of fear of reprisal and retaliation rather than because she was excited, inspired, or motivated by her work. Recognizing how stagnant and unmotivated she felt, she quickly moved to an organization where she felt the leader had a less rigid "personality" and leadership style.

Autocratic leaders are goal-driven and goal-oriented; they achieve team and organizational goals and tasks, but often at the cost of talented employees. Briefings Publishing Group describes the financial impact of employee turnover on companies when they write, "Turnover and absenteeism cost U.S. companies billions of dollars each year in lost productivity, recruitment costs, training costs, and lost opportunities." Autocratic leaders must remember that colleagues and employees are an organization's greatest asset and must be treated in a way that reflects their importance. Marlene's autocratic leader motivated through fear and intimidation. He got things done for his organization, but what did his aggressive and unwelcoming attitude cost his organization? His aggressive, unfriendly, and overbearing autocratic style cost him valuable employees and his best talent, like Marlene, who eventually left the organization to work for a competitor.

Pros of Autocratic Leadership

- Task-motivated leader.

- Clarifies expectations.

- Sets goals for each team member.

- Increases organizational productivity and effectiveness.

- Effective with crises, deadlines, and emergencies.

- Extremely efficient with time.

- Believes in workplace responsibility and accountability.

Cons of Autocratic Leadership

- Task-motivated leader.

- Dominates teams' interactions.

- Micro-manages team.

- Stifles creativity, team ideas, innovation, and opposing views.

- Lowers team morale in the long term.

- Creates fear and mistrust.

- Takes credit for team results.

- Increases turnover rates.

- Contributes to employee absenteeism.

- Engages in one-way communication.

Democratic Leadership

Democratic leaders promote team interests; she or he believes in and practices team involvement. Team participation, team participation, and more team participation are at the core of the democratic leadership philosophy.

Democratic leadership complements relationship-based leadership because the core foundation of this style is building cohesion and collaboration among colleagues, employees, and teams. Relationship-based leaders thrive when they've established and built significant interpersonal relationships with their colleagues and employees. The team's relationship motivates the democratic leader, who believes that building relationships and connecting personally and professionally with colleagues and employees are key to motivating, inspiring, and influencing a team to accomplish the organization's agreed-upon goals.

Using the democratic leadership style, Bill Gates turned Microsoft into one of America's most premiere organizations in less than three decades while making himself the wealthiest man in America, according to *Forbes* Magazine. *In What the Best CEOs Know*, international bestseller Jeffery A. Krames discusses Gates' leadership style and how, through team communication and participation, he built Microsoft into the powerful information-based organization we know today. Creating an environment that fostered open communication fueled Microsoft's growth, "...Gates often speaks about a culture that encourages the entire workforce not only to think, but also to share their thoughts with coworkers and managers up and down the company hierarchy." Gates wanted

© 2003 Ted Goff

"Isn't this what teamwork is all about? You doing all my work for me?"

to hear both the good and the bad news because both were important to the organization's continued success. "Bad news must travel fast," Krames quotes from Gates, who insists on accessibility to all information for all employees to ensure company growth.

Most leaders only want to hear the good or great news and frown at hearing the bad news, but awareness of bad news helps companies grow and develop from good to great, just as Bill Gates has demonstrated through his democratic leadership. Being aware of bad news allows organizations to correct what might not be working for colleagues, employees, and clients. I hope that you encourage your clients, colleagues, and employees to share the good, the bad, and the ugly news.

Democratic leaders also believe in shared decision-making and giving the team credit for its successes. Those working under a democratic leader usually find themselves working in a safe and friendly environment where participation and involvement are welcome, encouraged, and undoubtedly expected. Communication should go in both directions, and feedback should be frequent, positively oriented, and constructive. The leader, in a neutral and democratic fashion, mediates conflicts when they occur. Democratic leaders also believe in the *Principle of Equifinality, which is the ability of a team to accomplish an agreed-upon goal in many ways and from many different starting points.* In other words, a team or organizational goal can be accomplished in many different ways, but as a leader, you have to be willing to explore the various ideas and perspectives of your colleagues and employees to see how they would accomplish the goals. As the old saying goes, "There is more than one way to skin a cat." I believe it takes emotionally mature and team-centered leaders to fully listen to their colleagues' and employees' ideas, even when the leaders believe they may already hold the best ideas for the organization to implement. Listening to your colleagues and employees can be a constant challenge for many leaders, especially those who don't listen well or those who believe they are right all the time, but active and empathic listening are *essential* attributes of a democratic leader. Renowned professional and leadership development trainer, Larry Wilson remarks on how *not* listening affects a leader's growth and development when he writes, "Knowing is the enemy of learning." When leaders believe they already have the answers, they stop asking questions, learning, and listening to their colleagues and employees. Can a leader build team and organizational trust without learning from and listening to their colleagues and employees? Absolutely not!

Working under a democratic leader can overwhelm or frustrate those unfamiliar with democratic workplace processes or practices and/or those workers accustomed to doing their assigned tasks, completing their requests, and following leaders' orders. They can feel as though the leader is weak, uncertain, and ambiguous or, perhaps, lacking the confidence and decisiveness of an autocratic leader. It may also seem like valuable time is being wasted on team discussion and collective decision-making at the expense of team efficiency and productivity. Some democratic leaders may fall into the traps of not taking *any* control of the team when problems arise or of not enforcing order when a deadline needs to be met or a timely decision must be made. Democratic leadership can foster disorganization and chaos if the leader cannot moderate team discussions properly for time or content. When a team cannot come to a consensus or if the leader does not curb a heated debate, employees become stressed and can lose sight of the team's and organization's purpose, vision, and goals.

Pros of Democratic Leadership

- Relationship-motivated leader.

- Shares decision-making.

- Gives the team credit for achievements and successes.

- Creates a safe and friendly team environment.

- Engages in 2-way communication.

- Provides frequent and positive, constructive feedback.

- Seeks team's participation, ideas, and involvement.

- Mediates team's conflict.

Cons of Democratic Leadership

- Can appear ambiguous and weak.

- Can appear indecisive.

- Discussions can be too overwhelming for some team members.

- Sacrifices productivity at times.

- Too much talking and not enough doing at times (or perceived so).

- Can be perceived as too easy-going.

- Can appear unorganized.

Laissez-Faire Leadership

Laissez-faire leaders allow the team to take charge of most actions and decisions. Laissez-faire leaders are known to lead teams that are highly matured, self-driven, self-motivated, and self-managed. The laissez-faire leader expects the team to set its own standards, practices, procedures, goals, and priorities to plan and achieve company goals. She or he sees the team as having valuable personal and professional talents. These talents are honored, respected, and valued; the team is allowed free reign to set its own goals. In highly-motivated team environments, the laissez-faire leader can improve team productivity by empowering and encouraging the team to be self-motivated. Colleagues and employees feel satisfied in a climate where open communication is encouraged, rewarded, and welcomed.

The concept of "knowledge workers" is being used increasingly in the corporate sector. Thomas H. Davenport explains in *Thinking for a Living* that, "Knowledge workers have high degrees of expertise, education or experience, and the primary purpose of their jobs involves the creation, distribution, or application of knowledge." In other words, knowledge workers think for a living. They are paid handsomely to help the organization distinguish and differentiate itself from the marketplace competition. Knowledge workers spend their workdays developing creative and innovative moneymaking ideas to achieve this admirable feat. Knowledge workers are not your traditional American nine-to-five workers; they may say, for example, that they are most creative, effective, and productive between six p.m. and one a.m. These workers don't like to be told what to do; a laissez-faire leader is thus ideal for knowledge workers. Individuals with varying and specific knowledge bases are brought together to solve complex problems and to create new products, services, and solutions for the organization. Laissez-faire leadership works well in these settings and with team members who are highly mature and highly entrepreneurial in mind and nature.

Laissez-faire leadership is also ideal for organizations that focus on direct sales and network marketing, such as Mary Kay, Tupperware, and other companies whose "employees" are independent consultants running their own businesses. It is essential that each businesswoman or businessman be allowed to create her or his own purpose, vision, and goals; freedom is what allows markets to grow and expand. A Mary Kay consultant may be a work-at-home mom who organizes paperwork while her child naps, makes deliveries while taking her children to and from school, and calls clients just after dinnertime. On the other hand, someone in network marketing creates communication solutions between businesses in a region or city or because of similar goals. This person might run conference calls while on a bus or train; organize meetings at a local coffee shop during breakfast,

"We need to work harder, smarter and better. I'll be back after my vacation to see how we're doing."

brunch, or lunch; or spend hours driving to meet clients on different days. While these workers do not have daily office interactions or assigned tasks, they still need leaders to help them set goals, to provide them with resources, and, most definitely, to compliment their efforts.

However, if taken too far, a laissez-faire leader can appear detached, incompetent, indecisive, and withdrawn. A team without any relationship-based leadership can fall apart because it lacks solid focus, direction, and guidance even in laissez-faire organizations. Without a helpful leader and appropriate involvement, team members may find little motivation for creative and innovative thinking; they may lack resources or feel detached from a larger picture. Knowledge workers aren't simply driven because they have the autonomy and liberty to work creatively and innovatively; they want their creative ideas to be recognized by their leader and implemented by the organization. They want to reap the rewards of their efforts. Even Bill Gates implements knowledge workers' best creative and innovative ideas when he says, "Smart people anywhere in the company should have the power to drive an initiative." Most entrepreneurs and knowledge workers love creating new ideas, concepts, and products to bring to the marketplace and to advance their organizations. Even so, entrepreneurs and knowledge workers within organizations still need the experience, guidance, and structure that relationship-based leaders provide to their teams as they strive to meet the company's purpose, vision, and goals.

Pros of Laissez-Faire Leadership

- Honors and respects team member's personal and professional talents.

- Allows colleagues and employees free reign to set their own goals.

- Increases productivity and overall satisfaction in highly-mature and motivated teams.

- Creates a climate where open communication is encouraged, welcomed, and rewarded.

Cons of Laissez-Faire Leadership

• Leader can appear incompetent.

• Leader can be seen as indecisive.

• Can potentially decrease quality and quantity of team's work.

• Motivation is decreased with a completely "absent" leader.

• Innovation is decreased at times.

• Creativity decreases at times.

• Team members can feel isolated from their leader.

Real-World Challenge: You've inherited the leadership of the public relations division of a large corporation. Someone tells you that the previous leader was very autocratic and frowned upon others sharing ideas. What should you say at your first team meeting to ease the transition toward your leadership style, which is quite different from what they are used to?

Which Leadership Style Is Best?

A leader can come to a team with her or his individual fixed communication style, leadership style, and personality type. If you are that leader, it's a good idea to take stock of your own T.A.G.S. (Talents, Abilities, Gifts, and Skills) before you begin, so that you can embody and practice a leadership style that most effectively matches your team needs, wants, and expectations.

Research clearly shows that, in most cases, the democratic style is the most effective and will bring about the best and highest productivity and satisfaction among colleagues and employees. As you reread the section on democratic leadership, pay close attention to those attributes you have within yourself and those which need to be developed, nurtured, and practiced through an extra commitment from you. With you as an effective democratic leader, your team has the potential to be creative, optimistic, and vital. On the other hand, it is important to keep as many tools available as possible. Although democratic leadership is preferred, there might be times when you are on a high priority deadline that requires you be more task-oriented or autocratic while if you are a team leader for entrepreneurs or knowledge workers, laissez-faire leadership might be the best style for the situation.

Ultimately, in any team, you must find a *match* between your own leadership style and personal T.A.G.S. as well as those of the people you plan to lead. You first need to assess carefully the situation and environment in which your team works currently. How democratic can you be when your colleagues have not learned the communication skills you expect from them? Is this an environment where other leaders are acting quite differently from you? What exactly does your organization, your colleagues, and your employees expect from you? Are there times when you need to change your leadership approach? Answers to these questions require that you learn as much as you can about your colleagues and employees—their past experiences, their skills, and the communication styles to which they have become accustomed. Be patient and draw them into you without losing their respect, trust, and confidence.

"Get a Job at McDonald's if You Don't Like the Way I Lead"

Marlin Bogart was the Director of Information Technology for Stress Free Computer Services. His computer support staff of thirty-nine front-line workers didn't like his leadership style, which combined aggressive communication and autocratic leadership. Marlin was known for telling his team members frequently to "Go get a job at McDonald's if you don't like what I'm doing around here!" His thirty-nine colleagues and employees began to despise how he used fear, intimidation, and threats to accomplish his personal and professional goals in the workplace. After experiencing 6½ years of emotional and verbal abuse, the senior vice president of the company, Wendy Welcoming, finally terminated Marlin.

Wendy assumed responsibility for Marlin's duties before hiring a new director because she wanted to personally work at increasing the IT department's team morale and motivation. Her style combined assertive communication and democratic leadership. Wendy listened, smiled, respected others' opinions, encouraged feedback, and encouraged team participation, but she found herself feeling speechless and wounded professionally when the thirty-nine team members didn't respond favorably to her attempts to create a positive environment. She assumed that they would be elated to finally have a safe, positive, and supportive work environment. She failed to understand that for $6^1/_2$ years, the thirty-nine employees worked in an unsafe and low-trust environment marked by Marlin's regular screams, threats, profanities, and eye-piercing looks if they disagreed with his direction. Wendy had inherited a team of abused professional colleagues and employees who were reluctant to trust the administrators and executives of Stress Free Computer Services.

It took Wendy close to eighteen months to build credibility and win her colleagues' and employees' trust. What's the guiding principle of this story? Whenever a leader inherits a team of abused professionals, she or he must be patient because trust is built and established one interaction at a time.

Relationship-based leadership is definitely an art. When colleagues and employees are wounded in the workplace, an interim or new leader cannot legislate or mandate trust, because building and cultivating trust is a delicate interpersonal process. *You cannot rush the trust process.* Building trust requires respectful communication, time, hard work, and patience. Wise leaders assess their potential or current leadership environment to understand what has happened prior to their arrival. Although some will argue and say, "let bygones be bygones, and let's move forward," the reality remains that some colleagues and employees need an acknowledgement, a formal apology, or both before they can move on personally and professionally (whether or not you were the leader causing the turmoil and challenges). Relationship-based leaders ask the question, despite how *I* feel personally about the matter, how can *I* help my colleagues and employees move forward after a difficult workplace disaster?

ARE YOU THE RIGHT MATCH FOR THE LEADERSHIP POSITION?

Have you ever worked with someone in a leadership position who was incompetent? Do you and your colleagues despise working for an unprepared leader? Probably so! *Leading with Greatness* implies that a leader is ready, willing, and able to lead an organization successfully. I would like for you to consider the following four variables for determining whether you are in the right leadership position within your organization:

1. Understand your T.A.G.S. (Talents, Abilities, Gifts, and Skills).

2. Assess the situation or environment in which you are leading.

3. Assess your colleagues' and employees' T.A.G.S.

4. Understand the needs and expectations of the organization, your colleagues, and your employees *before* you accept the position.

In some cases, you may not be the right match for a particular leadership position or environment. When you assess your T.A.G.S., you have to be honest with yourself about your ability to meet the job criteria and expectations. Have you asked, "Why is the current leadership position vacant?" Have you considered that you may be leading in a toxic work environment where you are doomed to fail from the start? When choosing a leadership position, you must also consider team members' T.A.G.S. to ensure members can meet organizational goals. As a leader, you are only as successful as your team. As a relationship-based leader, you have two choices: (1) adjust your T.A.G.S. to fit the organization's expectations and requirements; or (2) determine whether the position is really meant for you. Would your T.A.G.S. be better used elsewhere? Will assuming this leadership position make you and your colleagues and employees unhappy? Are you capable of performing the expected duties? Is this the kind of environment in which you feel comfortable leading? Do your communication, leadership, and personality styles match the organizational culture? Are you setting yourself up for personal and professional failure? You should answer these questions to determine whether or not you should assume a particular leadership position.

Play to Your T.A.G.S. (Finding Your Perfect Career Match)

Earlier in my life, I held a corporate position as a district sales manager and earned the most money I had ever made in my professional career. Not long into the position and after saving $10,000, I quit and took an intrapersonal and introspective journey because I was unhappy professionally. Approximately three years later, I finally honored one of my spiritual callings by entering the teaching profession. I was offered a full-time college teaching position, and I was extremely excited. Although it was much less pay than my healthy corporate salary (plus a gracious expense account and bonuses), I was happy to be doing what I loved and what I knew the Creator had called me to do. I taught at a community and technical college for three years, and I was doing quite well in my new position. I was on the verge of becoming a tenured faculty member. The students, faculty, professional staff, and administrators loved what I was doing inside and outside the classroom. As a faculty member, I provided the institution with positive publicity in the greater Minnesota area through my professional consulting and speaking engagements.

At the college, I was known for teaching the late afternoon and evening courses. My daily ritual was to have soup and salad before teaching the long three-to-four hour evening courses. One evening before class, as I dined in the cafeteria, a senior administrator joined me for dinner and began to fill my mind with "ego food." He told me how I was a great addition to the college, a great leader on campus and within the greater Minnesota community, and how blessed and fortunate they were to have me as a faculty member. I kept thinking, "I really love this dude!" Forget cloud nine, I was on cloud 1,000. Immediately after the excessive compliments, he strategically and gently slid me a job description for the position of Associate Dean. He said, "Jermaine, I know you can do this job with ease. It would be a piece of cake for you, and we can increase your salary by

40%, if not double it." I drifted immediately and temporarily, and began to fantasize and romanticize about my dream house, my dream cars (a fully-loaded Mercedes Benz and a Range Rover), lavish shopping sprees, and spontaneous global travels. After this small fantasy stint, I came back to reality, and I said to the senior administrator that I would have to decline the position because I knew I had already found my professional calling as a teacher. The senior administrator tried his best to persuade me, but I knew within my heart, soul, body, and mind that I was supposed to be teaching and not doing college administrative work. One year later, I won the prestigious *Quality Instructor of the Year Award*. I never would have won the teaching award if I had accepted the position as Associate Dean. I would not have been playing to my T.A.G.S. had I accepted the job as Associate Dean, so instead, I continued to play to my teaching strengths.

Playing to your T.A.G.S. poses a dilemma, because people struggle between what they believe they should be doing and what others tell them they should be doing. When you play to your T.A.G.S., you are happier as an individual, and the organization becomes happier and healthier. I believe individuals are more successful overall in life, school, and work when they use their T.A.G.S. This fact reminds me of a statement by Dr. Dennis P. Kimbro, author of *What Makes the Great, Great* that says, "When you're doing what you love, your work is your play and if your work is your play you will never have to work a day again in your life." Are you playing to your personal and professional T.A.G.S. as a leader? If not, then you may not be developing your full potential as an effective relationship-based leader.

THE P.V.G. THEORY

The P.V.G. Theory aims to maximize and strengthen the effectiveness of any organization or team that follows the plan the theory proposes. The initials P.V.G. stand for the terms *purpose*, *vision*, and *goals*. Let's see how defining these terms, as they exist in organizational settings, can benefit everyone working under them.

Purpose

Purpose means having a complete and comprehensive understanding of your organization's mission. Do you know the fundamental reasons why your organization was created and established? Defining your mission requires care and specificity. For example, a hospital might have as its mission statement, "To help people." While the content is accurate, it is by no means complete, nor is it comprehensive. Teams who define their purpose need to think broadly about their reasons for being there, about those whom they serve and about those who will benefit from their work, products, and services.

It is your responsibility as a relationship-based leader to communicate constantly, consistently, and routinely the organization's purpose and vision so that there is no confusion about the company's purpose. The organization's purpose should be discussed so much that when conflicts surface or resurface in the workplace the discussion of the purpose becomes second nature. This reminder will return everyone's focus to why they are there in the first place. Even Jack Welch, former chairman and CEO of the General Electric Company, who increased GE's market capitalization by $400 billion, declared the importance of colleagues and employees knowing and understanding the organizational mission. In *WINNING*, Welch writes, "There were times I talked about the company's direction so many times in one day that I was completely sick of hearing it, myself." True, too much of anything may not be good. Excess repetition can and will kill the message and the messenger. However, organizations can make mission and purpose statements regular weekly agenda items, so long as this is done in a way that doesn't bore and annoy your team. Many colleagues and employees forget about the entire organizational picture when they get too involved in their day-to-day work routines. Your job as a relationship-based leader is to provide colleagues and employees with friendly reminders of the organization's purpose, vision, and goals.

Every organizational initiative, whether small or large, should always be connected to the organization's mission. When discussing an organization's mission and purpose, leaders should address and answer the following questions:

- **Why are we in business?**
  (the reason for the organization's existence or start-up)

- **What are we all about?**
  (knowing thoroughly what you do as an organization)

- **What are we providing?**
  (knowing completely your products and/or services)

- **Who are we serving?**
  (identifying and knowing your customers and clients)

I feel so strongly and deeply about all team players collaborating to move the organization forward that I've built activities around understanding mission and purpose in my *Leading with Greatness* workshops. I can't even begin to tell you how many times I've worked with people in various organizations where every member had a different perception of the company's purpose and mission. Stephen R. Covey, Ph.D. validates my consulting experiences in *The 8th Habit* when he quotes a Harris Interactive Poll of 23,000 full-time U.S. workers:

- Only 37% said they have a clear understanding of what their organization is trying to achieve and why.

- Only one in five was enthusiastic about their team and organizational goals.

- Only one in five workers said they have a clear "line of sight" between their tasks and their team and organizational goals.

Organizational chaos and conflict is driven often by ambiguity and confusion about the company's purpose and mission. If only 37% of colleagues and employees know what's happening in an organization, then 63% of employees are unclear and confused about how to move the organization forward. I'm not sure about you, but that's extremely frightening to me, not to mention a waste of company, stakeholder, and shareholder time, money, and resources.

All leaders, managers, and professionals responsible for recruiting and hiring should make discussing the mission and purpose of the company with all potential employees a standard company and job interview practice. It is a wonderful idea, too, to send a copy of the company's mission statement via mail, fax, or e-mail to all interviewees prior to all interviews. While interviewees are waiting in the reception area for the interview to begin, I believe they should be given another copy of the mission statement. By doing this, you expose the candidate to the values of the organization and help them make a decision about whether the organization is a fit for them. Of course, I believe in hiring the right person for the right position for the right company the first time around; this is smart and proactive hiring. Briefings Publishing Group believes hiring the wrong person can cost an organization three times the annual salary of the wrong new hire. They write, "The stakes are high when you're recruiting. Hire the wrong $50,000 employee and it will cost you $150,000. The wrong $150,000 employee costs you $450,000. That's for starters. There's also lost opportunity cost…plus lost business, potential customers, and momentum." If a candidate decides that your organization is not a good fit, there is no need for you to feel helpless and hopeless. Just remember the wise words of my grandmother, Margaret Ann Davis, "Don't be mad they left. It's going to save you many headaches in the long run." Just ask yourself how much a bad hire costs your organization. It is difficult to deliver excellent customer service and maintain business success if your colleagues and employees don't know what product and services your company is providing or why you're providing the services you do. This is why a company's purpose is essential to the P.V.G. Theory and to the company's ultimate success.

Vision

Helen Keller once wrote, "It is a terrible thing to see and have no vision." *Vision means having a clear mental picture of where you are headed as a leader and as an organization.* The organization's vision is derived both from the leader and from the input of colleagues and employees at all levels within the organization (this is an excellent example of democratic leadership). Like its purpose, a company's vision needs to be clear, understood, and achievable by all. It is the leader's responsibility to paint a crystal-clear picture of the organization's vision into the hearts and minds of each employee so all are clear on the direction in which the organization is moving.

Relationship-based leaders must paint a crystal-clear picture of the organization's direction. Your colleagues and employees must be able to see, hear, taste, touch, and smell the vision of the organization regularly. Relationship-based leaders must illuminate the vision in the minds and hearts of all team members and enliven it, so that colleagues and employees become enthusiastic and excited about it. Tobias and Tobias discuss how to make a vision stick with colleagues and employees in *Put The Moose On The Table* when they write, "To make a vision stick, at least two very critical components must exist. The vision must be crystal clear. But even when it is, you cannot simply order people to 'believe.' For a vision to take hold, it must also be compelling." Without discussion and personal connections to the vision, employees will have nothing to aspire to. This is why George Washington Carver wrote these fitting words, "Where there is no vision, there is no hope." Vision propels motivation, and lack thereof equals a team of bewildered, confused, distracted, and lost employees functioning minimally. Why? In the absence of vision and direction, employees don't know what to do, where to go, or in what direction to move. This is why leaders must articulate their team and organizational vision effectively and regularly. I suggest you paint the picture of your organization's vision as if you were Leonardo da Vinci, Henry Ossawa Tanner, Vincent van Gogh, Frida Kahlo, Georgia O'Keefe, or Pablo Picasso—in whatever style, manner, or color your colleagues and employees need to see it. By painting a crystal clear picture, this critical second component to the P.V.G. Theory will pay off with team clarity, direction, satisfaction, and motivation.

Goals

Goals are agreed-upon targets that leaders, colleagues, and employees direct their efforts and energies toward. Once you are armed with a fully-understood purpose and a vivid vision, you can begin setting individual and team goals strategically and collaboratively. Taking a larger vision and dividing it up into realistic target goals reveals the pathway the team needs to travel to fulfill the vision. Knowing the target goals gives each team member confidence, a solid sense of direction, and optimism about the team's future.

Leaders have to ensure everyone knows exactly the organization's daily, weekly, monthly, quarterly, and annual goals. All goals and tasks should be broken down *incrementally* to reduce the feeling of being overwhelmed. Overwhelmed colleagues and employees tend to procrastinate or avoid the goal or task completely. I suggest breaking all tasks into smaller goals and matching the right colleague and/or employee with the right goal or task.

A good question for leaders to consider is this: after the team has selected a goal to direct their efforts and energies towards, what resources will this person, team, or department need in order to achieve and accomplish this goal? If the individual or team hasn't been equipped with the correct tools and resources, the goal cannot and will not be achieved. This situation gives birth to what I call the *Nasty Evil Spirit of Procrastination, which is the art of perpetually putting off and postponing priorities until later.* Colleagues and employees procrastinate for many reasons. However, when goals or tasks are perceived as too large or too overwhelming, research among college students and career professionals shows that most people willingly give in to the Nasty Evil Spirit of Procrastination. Leaders must provide their colleagues and employees with the necessary tools and resources to complete organizational goals and tasks. Failure to achieve is most often due to a lack of strategy or resources to complete the task, and not due to a lack of will or skill on an employee's part. Employees who do not achieve company goals cost your company money and resources daily, weekly, monthly, quarterly, and annually. Setting reasonable, attainable goals and helping colleagues and employees accomplish them is vital to the P.V.G. Theory.

Real-World Challenge: You were recently promoted to leadership status over a team of colleagues you worked side-by-side with until last week. Can you expect these people to see you as their leader right away? If not, how do you facilitate this process?

LEADING A TEAM:
THE BENEFITS AND THE HEADACHES

Much of what I'm contributing to in this section I learned when I conducted a series of focus groups with Century College students. Each focus group's purpose was to gain a deeper insight into how participants felt about various team dynamics. These focus groups clearly revealed that while teams can be fun and functional, leading such teams requires finesse and hard work. In general, relationship-based leaders are great leaders because they enjoy working with teams of people striving to achieve common goals. Relationship-based leaders discover—mostly through time, experience, and trial and error—there is a definite art to motivating, inspiring, and influencing colleagues and employees. Great leaders pay a price to become great leaders. They enter a world where colleagues and employees have diverse perspectives, innovative ideas, and various opinions to share and debate. As a relationship-based leader, you get to share the organizational workload by delegating tasks based on your colleagues' and employees' T.A.G.S. (Talents, Abilities, Gifts, and Skills). As I mentioned earlier, knowing who your colleagues and employees are, what motivates them, and what they do best is the key to your success. It is important to create and maintain synergy. When a team is synergistic, everyone is enthusiastic and productivity soars in a friendly and cohesive work environment.

What is synergy, and how does one create it? Synergy derives from the Greek word sunergos, which means, "working together." Workplace synergy occurs when colleagues and employees communicate and work together as a united front. *Synergy occurs when the total sum of the team's effort is greater than the effort of each individual team member.* Synergy occurs when colleagues and employees collaborate. A synergistic team understands that organizations get further and accomplish more through team collaboration rather than individual effort. A relationship-based leader creates an environment that nurtures open communication and trust. Creating this environment leads to effective communication, cooperation, and synergy.

A pleasant, cooperative work environment is the ideal for which every leader strives. In practice, however, working as a relationship-based leader can be anything but ideal. Your colleagues and employees may have unmanageable personality differences with you or with one another. Some may be "slackers" who have already decided for themselves that the vision is unachievable or that the target goals are impractical. Such people appear lazy when, in reality, they are simply jaded and don't want to work on a project in which they don't believe. Remember what Dr. Covey found in his research, "Only 1 in 5 workers are excited about the team's and organization's goals." How would this statistic manifest in an organization of 500 employees? 100 employees would be excited about implementing ideas, pursuing certain markets, or developing specific products and services to grow the organization. On the other hand, 400 employees would be overly critical, cynical, or outright apathetic. Now, ask yourself how much market share, productivity, time, energy, payroll, company expenses, and stress these 400 employees can cost your organization. Can you really lead with greatness when 400 colleagues and employees aren't excited about organizational goals? I think not! Some team members may not have developed adequate trust in you yet, perhaps because until two weeks ago, you worked side-by-side with someone who is now your subordinate. These obstacles and resentments can make working with a team arduous, unproductive, stressful, and frustrating.

Leaders often encounter the *"groupthink" problem, which is the deterioration of individual decision-making as a result of group pressure.* Groupthink occurs when individuals within organizations deliberately minimize or altogether stop sharing their personal and professional perspectives with their team or organizational leaders and colleagues; they give in to the team's dominant thoughts. The agreed upon thoughts of the team may make individual members with opposing views *feel* like they *must* conform. Those who capitulate do so out of fear of career retaliation, fear of being passed over for advancement or promotion, or fear of being attacked and ostracized. Groupthink is dangerous. People lose their individuality, and organizations suffer because no one on the team discusses the potential dangers and negative consequences of team members' actions, ideas, issues, and decisions.

Engleberg and Wynn discuss how groupthink can lead to organizational and societal disaster in *Working in Groups*. They write, "…groupthink…a significant cause of the Challenger disaster. The Space Shuttle Challenger disaster occurred on the unfortunate morning of January 28, 1986. The Challenger exploded and ignited into unbearable flames 73 seconds after take off due to the failure of an ice-cold O-ring seal in the right solid rocket booster (known as the SRB). The seal caused a fatal leak which lead to the death of all seven crewmembers. When NASA officials ignored negative data and critics refused to seek or listen to outside expert opinion, and failed to examine all alternatives, they became classic victims of groupthink." This is also a classic example of the dangers of hubris-based leadership.

With an avalanche of American corporate scandals, it is apparent that organizations desperately need leaders and employees of integrity (those who do the right thing when no one else is looking). It doesn't take 100 employees or a dozen leaders to tarnish or destroy a company's reputation. It only takes one or two employees or leaders submitting to groupthink to sabotage the success of a reputable and respected organization. With that said, Enron is a modern-day example of hubris and of leaders failing to lead with integrity. As featured in *USA Today*, "The company (Enron) remains a symbol of corporate greed and hubris and one of the costliest U.S. bankruptcy reorganizations ever. Enron and other scandals spurred an unprecedented crackdown on corporate crime by prosecutors and regulators, who have nailed hundreds of defendants with fraud and other charges and hundreds of millions of dollars in penalties." Enron was a catalyst to the creation of the Sarbanes-Oxley Act, but they are not the only example of a business that lacked integrity. According to Economist.com and Forbes.com, here are other examples of American businesses in which groupthink tarnished the organization's brand and image:

Adelphia Communications	WorldCom
Arthur Anderson	Bristol-Myers Squibb
CMS Energy	Qwest Communications
Enron	Global Crossing
Halliburton	Harken Energy
Merck	Elan
Xerox	AOL Time Warner

Relationship-based leaders need to encourage team cohesiveness, but not excessive cohesion that pressures colleagues and employees to maintain uniformity at all costs. Team cohesion should never come at the expense of eliminating colleagues' and employees' ability to think freely and independently. Team cohesion between leaders, colleagues, and employees should be based upon mutual interests, common goals, respect, and trust.

PART FIVE

Leadership and Communication

Why is Communication So Important?

Communication is the number one tool humans use to navigate through life. Communication is the collective vehicle we use to build relationships. Communication is so vital to our mental, emotional, and physical well-being that its absence or presence affects our lives both positively and negatively. In fact, communication is so important that people who are isolated socially and withdrawn from other human beings are four times more susceptible to illness. Social isolates are also two to three times more likely to die prematurely than those with strong social ties, according to Adler, Proctor, and Towne in *Looking Out, Looking In*. "The type of relationship doesn't matter: Marriage, friendship, religious, and community ties all seem to increase longevity." People cannot get through life without communicating. One communication principle states that "You cannot *not* communicate." On a daily basis, whether we like it or not, we are walking, strolling transmitters, communicating and demonstrating our beliefs, emotions, and thoughts verbally and non-verbally.

My mother never told me that my success with others would be determined by the kinds of communication strategies and skills I employed. She never told me that my communication skills could either make, break, strengthen or weaken my relationships. I feel blessed to have found my calling of teaching leadership and communication skills to those who lead churches, colleges, corporations, and community agencies. I tell my students and workshop participants that, no matter what their major, career path, or program of study, everyone should enroll in at least two to three communication courses to improve their personal, professional, and intimate relationships. I meet many brilliant, wonderful, and talented leaders, parents, and professionals who often lack the ability to create positive communication climates. People can experience greater harmony in their personal, professional, and intimate relationships if they learn the art and skill of effective communication. Brian Tracy, author of the best-selling books *Maximum Achievement* and *The Psychology of Selling*, states, "85% of success in life is contained in one's ability to communicate effectively." Communication is the emotional glue that holds all relationships together.

Lack of communication from leaders leaves colleagues and employees uninformed about what's really happening inside and outside of the organization. Left to their own interpretations, colleagues and employees tend to reach their own conclusions and engage in workplace gossip. *Gossip is an unhealthy, unnecessary, and unproductive form of communication that negatively affects people and organizations.* However, most gossip within organizations can be reduced greatly or even prevented with assertive and effective communication from proactive leaders and employees.

My operational definition of effective communication is the ability to connect with listeners while conveying your ideas clearly and respectfully. If you cannot convey your ideas effectively, you will fail as a leader. You cannot motivate, inspire, and influence colleagues and employees if they don't understand you. Colleagues and employees won't live out the organization's purpose, vision, and goals if they don't understand their leader, and they certainly won't trust a leader who doesn't communicate well with them. Tobias and Tobias write, "Without a shared vision that is compelling and truly embraced with passion, it's nearly impossible for any organization to be successful."

In *Communication Miracles at Work*, Matthew Gilbert writes, "In real estate, the three most important things are location, location, location. In organizational life, it's communication, communication, communication. It is the number one challenge of groups, both large and small. I have yet to work with a team, department or company that didn't have communication problems." Effective or ineffective communication will determine the level of success a leader experiences. If you have been a leader for any length of time, you've probably realized that your greatest individual assets are your communication skills. These skills help you exchange information with your colleagues and employees about tasks and are necessary for successful organizational functioning. Like every aspect of your leadership style, your communication style is unique to you and developed through experience, trial and error, observation, and practice. I have come to see communication as the glue all teams need in order to function. Without it, maximum productivity and team trust are less likely to occur.

How Does One Communicate Effectively?

For relationship-based leadership to work leaders have to be cognizant of the communication principles and strategies that work best to motivate, inspire, and influence colleagues and employees. Let's face it, you can communicate however you like, but not all communication strategies yield maximum results. Understanding the psychology of the communication process is pertinent to successful leadership and organizational growth. Learning to communicate appropriately, competently, and effectively is a skill anyone can learn and develop. While some people believe you are either born with great communication skills or you are not, as a communications professor, I can tell you that communicating effectively is a skill you can *most definitely* learn. Anyone can replace old and bad communication habits, patterns, and practices with new ones. Although changing habits can be challenging, exhausting, and difficult at times, if you commit yourself to growing and developing, you can correct dysfunctional communication habits. I once read a quote that said, "Change is inevitable, but growth is optional." So, will you or won't you grow as an effective communicator?

The ability to communicate effectively is what separates great leaders from good leaders. Relationship-based leaders who manage chaos and conflict and who can extinguish communication fires have the skills to take their organizations to the next level. Colleagues and employees want leaders who possess adequate communication and people skills to unify the team to achieve the company's goals. Terry Felber, author of *Am I Making Myself Clear? Secrets of the World's Greatest Communicators* states, "Over 80% of the problems people encounter at work are related to a breakdown in communication. If we could discover the secret to successful communication, we could avoid 80% of the challenges that occur in our professional lives." Matthew Gilbert reinforces Terry Felber's point when he writes, "A general survey of corporate executives conducted by the American Management Association, concluded that communication-related conflicts—including misunderstandings, value differences, personality clashes, broken promises and arguments over methods—take up nearly a quarter of their time!"

Renowned UCLA Professor Emeritus of Psychology Dr. Albert Mehrabian found that *93% of all messages are communicated non-verbally while 7% of a message is communicated verbally.* This fact is important for leaders to know because they spend an abundance of their time communicating and interacting with colleagues and employees. Relationship-based leaders have to be aware of the verbal and non-verbal messages they send in casual, formal, and informal settings. Dr. Mehrabian explained and described the *7%-38%-55% Rule*:

> **Albert Mehrabian's Three Elements of Communication**
>
> *7%* of a message is received and understood by choice of *words*.
>
> *38%* of a message is received and understood by tone of *voice*.
>
> *55%* of a message is received and understood by *body language*.

For leaders to communicate effectively with their teams, the three elements of communication must be congruent and complement one another. An incongruent message occurs when a leader says with words (7%), "I have an open-door policy where colleagues and employees can come into my office and share their concerns and ideas with me whenever I'm available," but if her or his voice or emotional tone (38%) sounds monotone, sarcastic, unconvincing, or uninviting, a confusing message has been sent to colleagues and employees. If the leader states the same phrase but with her or his arms folded in a defensive manner, she or he also sends a confusing and incongruent message. It is important for relationship-based leaders to have congruency with their words, tone of voice, and body language. If leaders only regard the words they use, they fail as effective communicators because they are only regarding 7% of their message. Tone of voice and body language (non-verbal communication) combined make up 93% of face-to-face communication, according to Dr. Mehrabian's study. Yes, colleagues and employees listen to your words, but they spend the majority of their time listening to the tone of your voice and observing your body language. Ask yourself: are you using your 7%, 38%, and 55% as effectively as you can as a relationship-based leader?

Communicating effectively and appropriately also means that a leader knows which communication style or strategy is most fitting for the environment, the relationship, or the occasion in which the communication takes place. Communicating competently means a leader is skilled in and knowledgeable about the four communication styles (which I will cover extensively later in this section) and knows how and when to use each style respectfully. Communicating effectively means a relationship-based leader can convey her or his ideas and simultaneously maintain a personal or professional relationship. In other words, the leader accomplishes her or his communication goals while keeping the relationship intact. Conversely, you and I both know people, such as autocratic leaders and aggressive communicators, who convey their ideas but destroy the relationship in the process. Effective communication is a strategic art. When organizational chaos and team conflict occur, communication must become more artistic and strategic.

As we see from communication research and data, relationship-based leaders must understand the importance of effective communication and become knowledgeable about *how* communication works or doesn't work. The more diverse an organization's communication styles, the higher the probability for miscommunication, chaos, and conflict. This means that colleagues and employees run a greater chance of not achieving resolution on workplace issues from time to time. As Dr. Covey says, "Over 90% of all communication problems are caused by differences in either semantics or perceptions. *Semantics means the way you define words or terms. Perception means how you interpret data.* Whenever people listen to each other with true empathy, that is, within the other's frame of reference, both semantic and perceptual problems dissolve."

Can you communicate appropriately, competently, and effectively in the midst of chaos, conflict, and confusion? Relationship-based leaders and skilled communicators who have invested time into learning and developing the skill of communication can! Are you willing to invest in your communication skills? As a leader, are you aware of your communication limitations and weaknesses? What about your communication assets and strengths?

EFFECTIVE COMMUNICATION
AND LEADERSHIP STRATEGIES

The Excellent Communication Philosophy

As a relationship-based leader, you can make communication with your colleagues and employees easier by understanding and embracing the following three points, which give excellent communication its foundation.

1) Always enter every communication interaction giving 100% to the conversation.

Relationship-based leaders commit to giving their undivided attention to every conversation by being fully engaged when communicating with colleagues and employees. Former President Bill Clinton was known for his ability to connect and communicate well with people from various age groups, ethnic backgrounds, cultures, and socio-economic classes. One CEO named Bill Clinton as her favorite leader in a *FORTUNE* Magazine article titled "How to Become a Great Leader" because of his ability to connect and communicate well. The CEO stated, "When you are introduced to him, it's as if you are the only person in the room." I call this attribute of a leader focused communication.

I often say that great communicators and relationship-based leaders must be able to focus 100% on the conversation at hand and on the individuals with whom they converse. Even President Abraham Lincoln acknowledged he knew the power of focused communication when he wrote, "When talking with others, I spend 1/3 of my time talking and 2/3 of my time listening." Giving a 100% commitment to every communication interaction *must* be the mindset you bring to your work environment. You want your attention and communication to be positive, undistracted, and undivided. You can accomplish this by using appropriate eye contact (being aware of and respecting other people's cultural beliefs), by listening carefully, and by showing your friendliness and approachability during every interaction. As a relationship-based leader, you want your colleagues and employees to know you are willing to listen to their ideas, opinions, and feedback. Amazing things can happen when a colleague or employee believes that a leader's interaction is sincere and that she or he is being heard completely, fully, and thoroughly. However, as a relationship-based leader, you should also know when you are too preoccupied to communicate with your team members appropriately, competently, and effectively. A mind preoccupied with frustration, stress, deadlines, previous interactions, or personal issues will affect how your colleagues and employees perceive you when you are communicating with them. It would be better to reschedule the team meeting (if possible) to a time when you can give 100% to the communication interaction without mental interruptions and emotional stressors.

2) Commit to understanding others first.

The urge to quickly grasp what a colleague or employee says to you and then to formulate your response rapidly is a colossal communication problem in Western culture. Americans live in a communication culture where more emphasis is placed on talking and being understood than on listening and understanding others. These communication norms and practices drive leaders and organizations into unnecessary conflicts. Most arguments or communication conflicts are handled improperly and remain unresolved due to a lack of communications training, ineffective listening, and disrespectful communication We generally need no special training to spill out our opinions, but we often need to spend time learning how to listen well. Even though you may feel like this is the hundredth time you've heard the same idea from the same person, take a deep breath, remain quiet, and discipline yourself to listen to what is *not* said as well as to what *is* said. When colleagues and employees repeat their message regularly, it is probably because they don't feel heard or understood by their leader and colleagues.

As a relationship-based leader, patience is a virtue. Delay judgment and consider your colleagues' and employees' ideas and opinions before you share your own. Stephen R. Covey developed the popular phrase, "Seek first to understand, then to be understood." If you embrace this principle, you will see a considerable increase in team participation and organizational buy-in when you attempt to implement new ideas and start company initiatives.

One Chinese proverb states, "To be heard, there are times you must be silent." The key to getting your colleagues and employees to listen to you, as a relationship-based leader, is to listen to their concerns, ideas, and issues first. When colleagues and employees see that you have listened to their concerns, ideas, and issues, they will be more inclined and motivated to listen to your concerns, ideas, and issues. You gain more influence when you allow colleagues and employees to vent and speak, so when it is your time to share, they are more willing to listen to your concerns, ideas, and issues. It's easy to become blinded by your own enthusiasm that you don't take the time to listen to others first. Relationship-based leaders discipline themselves to listen to colleagues and employees before they speak. They are willing to delay personal gratification if it means honoring and valuing others first to move the organization forward. Relationship-based leaders collect their colleagues' and employees' ideas and information and, whenever possible, give positive feedback to ideas that have merit or potential. Then, combining the collective team wisdom with their own ideas, relationship-based leaders share their thoughts in an attempt to be understood and to generate ideas that include pieces of what others have already shared (This is an example of win-win in practical application, a positive method of conflict resolution that I will discuss later in the book). Make sure you give individual and team credit to colleagues and employees who initially shared creative and innovative ideas in order to maintain their trust.

In *Ten Secrets of Successful Leaders*, Dr. Donna Brooks and Dr. Lynn Brooks discuss the danger and importance of acknowledging and not forgetting past and present team member ideas, "Senior leaders have big egos. If you're a new member of a team—whether through promotion or external recruitment—you can't 'blow up' the previous work of that team and then ask for their help to move your own projects forward." It is imperative for leaders, whether existing or new to the team, to give credit to deserving colleagues and employees. It is even more important for leaders to communicate the achievements of colleagues and employees throughout the entire organization. When leaders acknowledge the hard-work and achievements of past and present employees it provides three benefits: (1) it boosts employee and team morale; (2) it sends a clear message to everyone that the leader is not an intellectual thief and that she or he is willing to share the limelight; and (3) the team feels valued because the leader has recognized and acknowledged publicly their hard-work.

Committing to understand colleagues and employees is a purposeful practice in empathic communication and listening. *Empathy occurs when a person or leader sees how another sees, thinks how another thinks, and feels how another feels; empathy is defined as seeing things from another person's point of view.* Empathy implies that a leader or communicator will attempt to get as close as she or he can to another person's experience to be able to understand that person's perspective. As a relationship-based leader, you can increase your probability of resolving communication chaos and conflict when you understand others' perspectives. Some communicators and leaders become so entangled in their own feelings that they disregard their colleagues' and employees' feelings; resentment and conflict subsequently occurs. When leaders don't listen, they destroy alliances and relationships critical to the organization. Building relationships is the essence and foundation of *Leading with Greatness*. Listening respectfully to colleagues and employees and communicating that you value them fuels team participation and motivation. If you don't believe me, try motivating your colleagues and employees without listening to them. How successful would you be as a relationship-based leader? How far will you get as a leader without listening? Listening is essential to effective leadership—if you don't listen, your colleagues and employees won't trust you enough to follow your leadership. Not listening is a HUGE sign of disrespect. Do you disrespect your colleagues and employees by not listening to them?

3) Commit to being understood by others.

Hugh Prather once wrote, "For communication to take place it must transcend *you* and *me* and become *us*." If communication doesn't result in mutual understanding then communication has failed. In a team compromise, we may never get full agreement from everyone, but if everyone leaves understanding all perspectives, you've sustained team respect and participation. While the most favored result for relationship-based leaders would be absolute team agreement and buy-in, I encourage relationship-based leaders to realize that, at times, team understanding may be all they can obtain from colleagues and employees. Understanding is a precursor to agreement, so it is important that relationship-based leaders commit first to understanding colleagues and employees and then to being understood by them. Colleagues and employees cannot agree with you if they don't understand you. Think of how a leader is perceived when she or he works first toward understanding colleagues and employees rather than seeking team agreement. As relationship-based leaders, our goal is to achieve consensus before we try to lead our team towards the goal. It is important to never leave a situation without being fully understood. This doesn't mean your colleagues and employees have to agree with your perspectives; they simply need to understand them. Aim to make yourself understood, regardless of how colleagues and employees may feel about your perspective. Ponder these questions for a moment: How can you tell when colleagues and employees thoroughly understand your intended message? How do you measure whether you conveyed your message and ideas successfully? What do you do when colleagues and employees resist your ideas and do not buy into what you say? Asking yourself these questions should help you help others understand your message.

The C.P.R. Communication Model

In reality, when we communicate with each other, the way we engage is complex and multidimensional. For example, you may feel as though your communication style towards your team is fair when, in fact, your colleagues and employees think you give some employees preferential treatment. They may label you as a leader who shows favoritism. Without feedback and careful self-reflection, you might never realize you have behaved this way because of your communication blind spots. As a relationship-based leader, understand that it is possible to favor and embrace certain colleagues and employees while simultaneously disrespecting and mistreating others. Are you just, equitable, and consistently fair to all colleagues and employees? I believe the *C.P.R. Communication Model* can help you evaluate how you communicate. It will also help you uncover your communication blind spots. Let's explore the dynamics of the C.P.R. Model.

The Content Dimension

The "C" of the C.P.R. Model stands for content, which is the subject matter or topic being addressed and discussed. It answers the question: *what* is being communicated? Acquisitions, mergers, budget cuts, customer service issues, layoffs, sales forecasting, market expansion, diversity issues, hiring practices, promotions, or recruitment and retention are all examples of content dimension topics that many organizations discuss. In a team environment, the most effective communication happens when everyone knows the topic or material being discussed prior to the team meeting. Colleagues and employees can then prepare adequately for team discussion. Have you ever attended a meeting where several members didn't know what the meeting was about, so they couldn't prepare for the discussion in advance? This can make for a long, boring, time-consuming, and unproductive meeting. If you, as a relationship-based leader, fail to provide your colleagues and employees with necessary agendas, outlines, and pertinent background material prior to a meeting, you cannot expect them to produce quality results. Content is the backbone of dialogue and discussion. If your colleagues and employees don't know or understand what's being discussed, the discussion has no place to go, and the meeting becomes a waste of time. I encourage you to provide everyone on your team with content and context before your next team meeting.

The Process Dimension

The "P" of the C.P.R. Model stands for process, which involves *how* you *treat* colleagues or employees with whom you communicate and interact. Do you assign projects fairly and equitably? Do you disregard certain colleagues' and employees' ideas and opinions while you always celebrate and honor others' contributions? Do you say "hello" to some people but never make eye contact with others? Your effectiveness as a relationship-based leader depends on your ability to connect genuinely with and respect your colleagues and employees, to work with their T.A.G.S., and to create a work environment where each employee feels respected, valued, and vital to the team process and progress. It's also important that you don't tolerate behavior in others that lessens or demeans the value of another member of the team. Respectful treatment from everyone on the team goes a long way toward developing a pleasant and productive team and a healthy work environment.

The Relational Dimension

The "R", which is the relational dimension of the C.P.R. Model, means you are aware of how you *feel* about the colleagues and employees with whom you work, communicate, and interact. How do you relate to or not relate to your colleagues and employees? This dimension explains *why* you communicate the *way* you do with certain colleagues and employees. The personalities and cultural backgrounds of your colleagues and employees do not come in a "one size fits all" box. Too many leaders and employees allow their personal feelings and hang-ups to interfere with their professional commitments, duties, and expectations. Not liking a colleague or employee is no reason to be disrespectful, rude, and unfair. It takes discipline and emotional maturity to still be fair and respectful towards an individual you may not like. There may be colleagues and employees that you genuinely like and would consider your friends, even if you weren't their team leader. Other members of your team may not fit well or connect with your personality, communication, and leadership style. These colleagues and employees seem to always deal with team conflict and problems in exactly the opposite way you would choose to deal with them. If you are experiencing these types of challenges, there are two communication concepts worth exploring, known as the *Halo Effect* and the *Horn Effect*. *The Halo Effect and the Horn Effect means that when you like an individual you find yourself only able to see the good or positive in them, whereas, if you don't like someone, you can only see the bad or negative in them.* All are either angels or devils—halos or horns—in this figurative view. As a relationship-based leader, avoid this dysfunctional dynamic and behavior and be aware that while you may feel differently about various team members, you cannot appear so to the team. Professionalism without prejudice is a worthy goal. *Professionalism requires the performance of fair and equitable behaviors in the workplace even when you don't feel like it.* Relationship-based leaders adhere to and maintain professionalism to move the team and the organization forward.

Approximately 400 adults enroll in my communication classes annually; they embody various attitudes, personalities, cultural backgrounds, and communication styles. Ideally, a professor would treat all of her or his students equally. However, in the real world, this is not always the case. It doesn't matter if I like all of my students, but it *does* matter that I treat them respectfully as human beings, students, and customers of Century College. I maintain my professionalism by understanding my personal views cannot and *must* not interfere with my professional duties and expectations. If you model professionalism for your colleagues and employees, they will often share this perspective when dealing with one another.

The C.P.R. Model in Real Life

I taught the C.P.R. Model one evening for a course titled "Principles of Interpersonal Communication" to a group of professional adults transitioning into the healthcare field. I explained how we, as effective communicators and future relationship-based leaders within our chosen fields, have to become cognizant of the potential dangers stemming from the relational dimension of the C.P.R. Model. I really tried to emphasize the point that the relational dimension is the catalyst behind how we behave in the process dimension.

I explained that any negative feelings we hold towards colleagues and employees could lead us to discriminatory practices if we are not careful and cognizant of our personal biases and stereotypes. *[Discrimination is the denial of access, opportunities, and growth for individuals and groups, usually in the areas of banking, business, customer service, education, employment, housing, and politics.]*

© 2005 Ted Goff

"Fairness... fairness... I've heard that
word somewhere. What does it mean?"

This communication model explains why some companies make news headlines due to their discriminatory practices. However, it is not the organization that discriminates. Rather, it is the individuals in power positions within the organizations that discriminate against certain individuals and groups of people. The C.P.R. Model reinforces the idea of why some people within organizations are fired, not hired, never promoted, or never compensated fairly.

I was satisfied professionally when I taught my students the C.P.R. Communication Model because I was leaving them with a powerful message that all human beings need to hear, especially those in leadership positions. Immediately, I saw a hand go up (let's call her Jocelyn). I acknowledged her by saying, "Yes, Jocelyn," and she proceeded to say, "I have an excellent story that illustrates what you've been teaching, Professor Davis." I asked her to please share the story with the class. She said, "When I was working towards my first degree, I took an evening job at a 24-hour restaurant serving food so I could earn tips to pay my college and living expenses. I felt making tips was the best way to finance my way through college." Well, Jocelyn immediately found out that she would have to work the midnight to seven a.m. shift, which meant she would be encountering people who frequented the restaurant after the bars and nightclubs closed. The problem with this situation was that Jocelyn despised communicating and interacting with anyone who was intoxicated or even appeared intoxicated.

She said, "I hate drunk people." I asked, "Do you hate ALL drunk people?" and she said, "Yes, ALL drunk people!" I proceeded to ask why she harbored such a strong displeasure towards drunkards. She said that, without going into detail, both of her parents had been alcoholics throughout her entire life. Now, when I teach, I love to play Devil's Advocate in class to create controversy, excitement, fun, and sensation. So, I said to Jocelyn, "Well, there are some people who handle their liquor very responsibly while others are belligerent, loud, obnoxious, and wild when they drink. Do you treat the responsible drinkers disrespectfully, as well?" She said, "Yes, I do!" I then asked, "What if they are polite to you?" She paused and thought for a moment and said, "Maybe it's not the right thing to do, but I'm definitely not as friendly to intoxicated customers as I am to my sober customers."

I asked, "If a customer comes into the restaurant and she or he is acting in a congenial and respectful manner, but you smell a little beer, wine, or tequila on her or his breath, will you change the kind of customer service you provide to your patron?" She replied once again, "I'm not saying it's right, but I haven't been the nicest server to drunk and intoxicated customers because I don't like them due to my past and upbringing." I told her, "I understand, but I have one more question for you. Do you believe you are discriminating against the patrons of the restaurant when you provide rude customer service even to the intoxicated customers who are congenial and respectful?" She said, "I just never thought about my actions being on the border of being discriminatory." I told her, "Jocelyn, most people don't really think about how their feelings about other people can make a heaven or a hell for the person with whom they communicate and interact. You have just seen that no one is immune to those kinds of feelings." I finished the night by reiterating the benefits of understanding the C.P.R. Model and by admonishing my students to remember that, as future relationship-based leaders, they could not afford to practice inappropriate, unacceptable, and discriminatory behaviors toward anyone. I ended the class with a quote that evening stating, "Change begins with awareness. You cannot change what you are not aware of or what you are not willing to face."

BARRIERS TO EFFECTIVE COMMUNICATION AND LEADERSHIP

Ralph Waldo Emerson once said, "What you are speaks so loudly I cannot hear what you say." I've been teaching communication classes on college campuses for over

10 years, and I've learned that the intentions of most messages never reach the listeners effectively. However, as effective communicators, we can change that outcome by learning to eliminate the barriers, distractions, and noises that intercept our intended messages. While you may envision having a perfectly productive meeting with your team members, such an expectation is rarely practical if leaders are not knowledgeable about how effective communication takes place. Think of the 7%-38%-55% rule. How many leaders are unaware that 93% of their communication is nonverbal? The highest barrier to clear and effective communication is "noise." *Noise is any factor that prevents and interferes with your intended message, resulting in the message being misunderstood or not received by the intended listener.*

There are four kinds of potential noise in any communication setting that could prevent colleagues and employees from fully understanding and receiving your intended message as a relationship-based leader.

Physical Noises

Physical noises are external distractions in the physical environment, separate from the communicator or listener(s). Any noise in the physical environment can interfere with how your message comes across and with what your listeners actually hear. Another example of physical noise might be a smoke-filled room that distracts and irritates some listeners. There is a possibility that the physical noise could be coming directly from the listeners themselves. Cell phones, Blackberries, text messages, laptop computers, sidebar conversations, and interruptions can make for a chaotic and unproductive discussion, meeting, or lecture. As a relationship-based leader, it is your responsibility to recognize the presence of physical noise and distractions and attempt to eliminate the noise as quickly as possible in order to ensure effective and quality communication.

The "Nip It in the Bud" Factor

I was once invited to give two 45-minute keynote presentations at a high school in St. Paul, MN. The assembly hall held approximately 600 students. While trying to hold the attention of 600 high school students can be a daunting and difficult task, I held their attention

successfully, except for one group of three students who busily enter-
tained themselves and those around them. At one point, their laugh-
ter exceeded my message, and yes, they created physical noise and
distractions for me and anyone nearby who wanted to listen to my
speech. As a keynote leader, I knew I had to nip this one in the bud.
I gracefully eased over to the left side of the stage, stood there,
looked all three students directly in the eye, and said, "May the rest
of the auditorium join in your discussion because it appears to us
that you are all having a ball, and we want to have fun, also." I asked
the audience members if they agreed, the three students piped down,
and the audience members all applauded my leadership ability to
eliminate the physical noise and distraction that prevented my
intended message from being heard and understood fully.

Physiological Noises

*Physiological noises are biological distractions that occur within the communicator's
or listener's body which interferes with the intended message being received and
understood fully.* If you are tired, hungry, have allergies, a cold, back pain, or a
headache, you're not as likely to put forth extra effort into the communication
interaction. If you are physiologically worn down, sometimes it helps to share that
information with colleagues and employees at the beginning of the team meeting.
If they see there is a simple explanation for your abnormal behavior, they will be
less likely to think the worst or to wonder if they are responsible for the interaction being less than effective. The key factor for all of us is awareness of how our
physiological states can interfere with clear, effective, and quality communication
with colleagues and employees. When you know you are not functioning at your
normal state, you can tailor your behavior accordingly to communicate successfully with your colleagues and employees. The following story illustrates my point.

Should My Pain and Misery = Your Pain and Misery?

I have learned that my communication skills and perceptions become
screwed up when I am hungry, irritated, tired, or stressed. When I

have a stuffy head, an annoying cough, a sore throat, an aching back, or a sinus infection, I can become an extremely grouchy and horrible ineffective communicator. Here's what I've learned about myself as a communicator: if I don't monitor my behaviors when physiological noises are a problem for me, I become easily agitated and annoyed. My communication becomes abrupt, disrespectful, and rude; I am definitely less patient with colleagues and students. That sounds like the making of a great relationship-based leader, doesn't it? Can you imagine being in an all-day team meeting with me while I'm behaving and communicating in this awful manner? When relationship-based leaders are unaware of or disregard the impact of their physiology on their interpersonal interactions, they begin to create an unpleasant work environment, which, of course, is de-motivating and stressful for their colleagues and employees.

Psychological Noises

Psychological noises are the mental and emotional distractions within either a speaker or listener that can interfere with her or his ability to fully convey or understand a message. These noises are similar to physiological noises except that stress, interpersonal conflicts, depression, or simply being emotionally worn-out by conflict replace the physiological factors. For example, if your organization has recently made layoffs or budget cuts, this can become a stressor that affects everyone in the organization. When you find yourself feeling worn out, it is time to relax, take more breaks during the meeting, and generally take care of the team's mental and emotional needs. It is important to consciously separate these distracting feelings and emotions from the situation, which enables you to be a more effective communicator, listener, and relationship-based leader.

Help Me Understand Your Mood Swings!

Earlier, I mentioned that I work with 400 college students annually, and we get to know one another's characteristics and behaviors quite well because we see and interact with one another more than 30 times per semester. All human beings are creatures of habit, which means we all have certain behavioral patterns that we've adopted and use on a regular basis. I believe that if you really want to learn about people, you can ask them about themselves, or you can do what relationship-based leaders do—just watch and observe them in action, and look at what they do (remember the D.A.L.O. Approach). Why? Because actions speak louder than words. When you observe and watch others, you can read them as if you were reading a book.

Because my students communicate and interact with me at least twice a week, they've become familiar with many of my habitual and regular mannerisms. So, if I deviate from my normal patterns of action, my behavior raises a perceptual antenna in the minds of my colleagues and employees, and they are likely to assign meaning to my actions in an effort to make sense out of their observations. Social scientists describe this as "attribution theory." *Attribution theory is the process of attaching and assigning meaning to behavior.* When colleagues and employees can't make sense out of a leader's actions and behaviors, they eventually begin to assign meaning to those actions and behaviors. This assignation poses a predicament for the relationship-based leader, because her or his actions and behaviors are typically (and unfortunately) misconstrued or taken out of context, which leads to more team challenges, chaos, and communication problems. When colleagues and employees make inaccurate attributions, their subjective diagnoses limit the leader's ability to motivate, inspire, and influence her or his team. Two specific types of attribution errors can lead to miscommunication and conflict: fundamental attribution errors and ultimate attribution errors. Let's imagine that I have behaved out-of-character, and my team members notice that my behavior is out-of-character. When we act out of character, we tend to attribute external causes to the behavior ("I behaved that way because workplace conflict is so intense"). Others, however, notice our out-of-character behavior, and are more likely to attribute an internal (rather than external) cause ("He behaved that way because he's a mean person"). *Thus, fundamental attribution errors occur when others assign an internal cause to our behavior; ultimate attribution errors occur when we assign external causes to our own behavior.*

Since I understand the negative effect attribution errors can have on my ability to lead effectively, I've learned to communicate my psychological noise immediately to my colleagues and students when I'm stressed or preoccupied. I'm not saying relationship-based leaders have to spill their guts or open up their personal lives to their colleagues and employees, but communicating with them about your current level of stress or preoccupations can make a world of difference. You spend a significant amount of time around your colleagues and employees, and they have had a chance to get to know you over the months and years. By being open and providing clarification, you can quickly eliminate potential gossip. Communicating openly and honestly allows you to extinguish organizational fires before they become unmanageable. Sometimes I'll simply say to my students, "If I appear different today, it's not you at all; it's me." As a relationship-based leader, you can leave it there, or you can go further by saying, "You know last night was one of those nights when I didn't sleep very well" or "The dog pooped all over my brand new carpet as I was leaving out the door for work this morning." The goal is to use communication to close the assumption-making gap between what your team thinks and what is actually happening. Although we may believe our team members shouldn't take things personally, the reality is people *do* personalize actions and behaviors. That process usually works against the leader. Right, wrong, or indifferent—it happens. Do your colleagues and employees perceive you as a leader who deliberately withholds information from them? Is a lack of communication with your team creating a negative perception of you as a relationship-based leader? Communicating more clearly with your team can correct many of these misperceptions.

Speaker-Generated Noises

Speaker-generated noises and distractions occur when your personal attitude, behaviors, and disposition affect your message and how it is understood and received. Have you ever had a bad attitude or disposition? Have you ever behaved disrespectfully towards a colleague or employee while trying to communicate with her or him? If you have, your ideas and opinions more than likely failed to reach your intended listener because of your speaker-generated noise. As leaders, our communication fails at times because colleagues and employees choose deliberately to stop listening to us because of our speaker-generated noises and distractions. Yes, we, too, can obstruct our own messages. In other words, our attitudes and actions can be the central reasons for communication failure. There are several ways to make your colleagues and employees quit listening to you: disregard their opinions; disregard certain team members; act like a know-it-all; be sarcastic; minimize others' ideas; look uninterested; appear defensive; roll your eyes; click your pen or doodle while others talk; frown; yell; scream or be condescending to others; pseudo-listen; use profanity; and act as if you are superior to others.

If you're leading a team and you secretly hold a belief that your team members are inferior to you intellectually and professionally, your attitudes and actions will show it by how you talk to them and treat them. Even if you find yourself annoyed by just one or two members, the entire team can be affected as a result. Pay close attention to the tone of your voice (your 38%). It is also important to pay attention to your body language (including eye contact). Your body language (your 55%) is just as important, if not more important, as the words you say because 93% of communication is non-verbal! I attended a meeting where the female speaker was dressed provocatively; afterward, my female and male colleagues said they remembered what she wore but little of what she said. Be aware and take stock of how you present yourself to the team. Always ask yourself, "What is my 55% communicating and what is my 38% saying today?"

I Hear You, Momma, but I'm Not Listening!

As a single parent, my mother never hesitated to let me know that she was in charge and that she ran our household. She could be the nicest and sweetest mother ever, but when she became angry, she would transform into a loud cursing, screaming, and yelling menace. After I became a professor of communication studies, I went home to Chicago one summer to spend a little quality time with my mother because I really missed our heart-to heart-discussions. We were in the kitchen, and she was preparing my favorite dish: home-made macaroni and cheese (umm, umm, umm!). She surprised me when she proceeded to ask, "Jermaine, why were you so hard-headed and stubborn when you were growing up?" I replied, "Ma, are you serious? My behaviors were angelic when I was growing up!" We both laughed. Then she said, "No, I'm serious. Why didn't you listen to me? I was only trying to steer you in the right direction." I responded, "Do you really want to have this conversation?" and she nodded yes. I took a deep breath and said, "Okay, here's the truth. When I was growing up, I never heard, processed or listened to much of anything you said when you were cursing, screaming and yelling at me. I shut down mentally and emotionally as soon as I heard those first profanities come out of your mouth. I couldn't tolerate the screaming and yelling because it annoyed and angered me. I used to hate when you addressed me in that manner; it made me feel very little. I felt like you were disrespecting and devaluing me as your son and as a human being."

Of course, my mother had tried to convey pertinent and powerful messages; I simply couldn't process those messages because they were clouded by speaker-generated noise: cursing, screaming, and yelling. Those factors interfered with my ability to receive and understand her intended message. As a leader, when was the last time your speaker-generated noise interfered with your message being fully received and understood? What can you do to prevent speaker-generated noise from being a barrier in your relationships?

Side note: My mother passed away recently after a long, ugly, 2¹/₂ year battle with diabetes, and one of the things I miss most about Carolyn "Charmaine" Davis is that I could talk with her about anything—and I mean anything. I apologized to her for being a stubborn child at times and she apologized to me many times when I was younger because she felt she had failed me as a single mother. Yes, she was stubborn at times, but I miss my rich, real, and authentic talks with her. She was truly a very special woman to me. Thanks, Ma!

When it comes to eliminating distracting noises, remember this advice: (1) be aware of and eliminate distractions; (2) take personal time when necessary before responding immaturely or emotionally; (3) allow yourself to respectfully express your concerns; and (4) discuss difficult issues with your team to prevent resentment from developing among colleagues and employees.

LEARNING TO AGREE TO DISAGREE—
IS IT REALLY POSSIBLE?

Learning to deal with conflict peacefully is a difficult task, but it can be done. Colleagues and employees differ in personality, ability, communication style, and basic core values. You might find yourself in the tough position of leading a colleague or employee who doesn't agree with your ideas any more than you agree with hers or his. In the workplace, this situation doesn't have to create an indefinite stalemate or become the beginning of a feud. You and your colleagues must learn to agree to disagree effectively without resenting one another; this process involves *listening* carefully to what your colleagues and employees are saying and allowing adequate time for them to express themselves. Even if you don't agree with your colleagues or employees, it helps if you **understand their perspective.** Finally, **negotiate a plan** with your colleagues and employees as to how you will proceed after the conflict or disagreement. This involves a sincere dialogue between you and your colleagues and employees with the expectation that you can move forward in spite of a disagreement.

Points to Remember: Learning to Agree to Disagree

The next time you find yourself in a conflict or disagreement when you don't see eye to eye with a colleague or employee, please follow the 5 Steps of Learning to Agree to Disagree as a method of conflict resolution and unity building.

1) Seek first to understand, then to be understood.

You may recognize this point from the Excellent Communication Philosophy. The first point is this: always enter every communication interaction giving 100%. If you are dedicated to becoming a relationship-based leader, agreeing to disagree is an important skill to develop. Once you have put yourself in the proper mindset to understand your colleagues and employees you can then advocate for your own stance, now you are ready to communicate empathically to build strong cohesive work relationships. Giving 100% to the interaction means that you are completely engaged, present, and prepared to work towards mutual understanding and agreeing to disagree.

2) Establish the points of agreement.

What do you agree on? Find a common ground, and begin the conversation on a positive note. As a communicator and relationship-based leader your goal is to create an environment in which colleagues and employees feel safe enough to address real issues and problems. This is why acknowledging what issues and ideas you both already agree upon is so important. Doing so creates a positive tone and work environment for productive dialogue. Creating a safe workplace environment is key for colleagues and employees if you want them to be open and honest about difficult and uncomfortable topics. As a relationship-based leader you want to create a work climate where colleagues and employees are comfortable discussing the "undiscussable" topics that people and organizations typically avoid. Ask yourself, "Am I creating a safe and healthy communication environment for colleagues and employees so that they can navigate through difficult and uncomfortable dialogue while angry, fearful, upset, and frustrated?" Once you, your colleagues, and your employees have established mutual agreement, you can set a positive tone for communication to take place in a calm, respectful, and productive manner.

3) Establish the points of disagreement.

Oftentimes, disagreements become so heated and emotional that we forget what we are actually arguing about. Never allow yourself to get so swept away by your emotions that you forget what created the conflict or disagreement. The key to agreeing to disagree is being able to clearly identify and explain the conflict

or disagreement. A competent communicator and relationship-based leader should be able to articulate and communicate the conflict or disagreement in one sentence. I say one sentence because when people are emotionally-charged and on the verge of leaving their base-line, they are more likely to succumb to horrible listening behaviors; emotionally, they are too blind and preoccupied to pay attention. You can help your colleagues and employees focus by giving them a one-sentence problem rather than a one-or-two-paragraph problem. More than one sentence causes information overload.

Sorting Through My Emotions

I remember an incident when a family member that I also considered a good friend borrowed money from me. This person was unable to repay me when she promised; she began to avoid me as a result. Our friendship deteriorated, and I was hurt to say the least. I experienced many emotions: anger, sadness, surprise, aggression, disappointment, disrespect, helplessness, hopelessness, and vindictiveness. After I acknowledged these emotions, I attempted to carefully categorize them to understand why I was so hurt by her behaviors. I eventually focused on the four reasons why I was hurt: (1) I hated the feeling of someone avoiding me; (2) I felt disrespected because I believed my kindness was unappreciated; (3) I was hurt deeply because she abandoned our friendship, and I had enjoyed the company of this person more than anything; and (4) I needed my money (Imagine that!). It seemed as though the money was the point of disagreement, but when I took more time to reflect, I discovered that the real issue was the lost friendship; that loss formed the nucleus of my hurt. I had asked myself, "Jermaine, what's the real issue?" When I finally confronted her, I centered the conversation on the lost friendship, since that was the real point of disagreement for me. Once you establish the origin of the disagreement, you can take steps to amend and move forward. Please note that there need only be consensus regarding the fact that conflict exists; parties may still differ as to the nature, scope, or effects of the conflict.

4) Reassess your position after careful consideration.

Once you have listened to and understood your colleague or employee, once you have found common ground, and once you have discovered the real point(s) of disagreement, take time to process the information. You may find that your colleague or employee has a valid point. You still may not agree with her or his perspective, but you might shift your perspective as a result. Even if you are unmoved in your position after reassessment, the act of reassessing communicates that you are actively, deliberately, and purposefully exploring your blind spots and considering others' perspectives, which is a vital part of agreeing to disagree.

5) Negotiate a plan for how to proceed in spite of your disagreement.

At this point, you and your colleagues or employees should have a clear understanding on what you agree and disagree. This understanding should provide you with a foundation for planning how to move forward and achieve team goals. The disagreement should no longer be a roadblock in communication and team progress. Simply ask the colleague or employee how would you like to proceed from here? This question encourages all parties to become solution-based thinkers rather than problem-based thinkers. *Solution-based thinking forces colleagues and employees to be more creative and innovative when solving difficult workplace issues and problems.*

EMOTIONAL INTELLIGENCE: ABOVE ALL, KNOW THYSELF

Emotional intelligence is the awareness of one's own emotions and thought processes. Relationship-based leaders who lead with greatness are emotionally intelligent, while mediocre or poor leaders do not understand the concept of emotional intelligence and don't recognize the impact of their emotional or psychological states upon their leadership effectiveness. As mentioned earlier, a relationship-based leader can create noise easily if she or he is not aware of her or his physical, physiological, psychological, or speaker-generated noise. This noise can hinder effective communication from taking place and can send mixed messages to colleagues and employees and even turn them off to the leader's message.

Every person has a psychological and emotional "base-line" from which she or he naturally functions and operates. The further you move away from your base-line, the less able you are to communicate effectively and think rationally. It can be easy to become anxious, unsure, passive, or even aggressive if you have moved too far away from your base-line. When people become aggressive, they perceive that they have more control when, in reality, they have less control. Road rage is an example of how dangerous moving away from one's base-line can become. I remember reading a story about a physician in Minnesota who, because he was angry with an older woman driving slowly in the left hand lane, ran her off the road and then proceeded to get out of his car, go to her driver's side window, and punch her in the face. This was a doctor—a professional person and a community leader—functioning without emotional intelligence and acting out of his normal mode of operation, or at least what we think and hope would be his normal mode of operation.

What's Causing You to Leave Your Base-Line?

Many times conflicts and challenges move us away from our base-line. *A base-line is the normal emotional and mental state from which you function and operate.* Here are a few adjectives to describe various kinds of base-lines from which individuals function and operate: bubbly, extroverted, gregarious, happy-go-lucky, outgoing, upbeat, calm, defensive, gentle, introverted, laid back, relaxed, serene, and uptight. When relationship-based leaders are aware they are moving away from their base-lines, they are less likely to become emotionally explosive and destructive. As a relationship-based leader, your self-management begins with self-awareness. If you are not aware of your emotional temperament, you cannot manage yourself emotionally. Can you calm yourself down when you are aroused and agitated? Can you tell when you are about to erupt emotionally during a heated and out-of-control discussion? Can you tell when you are leaving your base-line, or can you *only* tell you've left your base-line *after* the damage is already done?

Adler, Proctor, and Towne describe *self-monitoring as, "The process of paying close attention to one's behavior and using these observations to shape the way one behaves."* Communicators and relationship-based leaders who are high-level self-monitors can usually tell and feel when they are moving away from their base-line, and if they act promptly and swiftly, they can prevent personal and orga-nizational chaos and conflict from transpiring. Conversely, low-level self-monitors are more likely to leave their base-lines and contribute to a dangerous, unhealthy, and toxic work environment. While dealing with conflicts is discussed in part six of this book, I want to look at what I call *"emotional* and *psychological triggers"* that, if you're not aware of them, can quickly pull you away from your base-line. You may have heard emotional and psychological triggers referred to as *"hot-buttons."* If others pull or activate these triggers or push your hot-buttons, you can simply "lose it" because you are functioning outside of your normal range of emotions. Emotional and psychological management begins with the personal awareness of our own triggers and hot-buttons. Do you know what triggers and hot-buttons cause you to move away from your base-line? There are four general categories of emotional triggers and hot-buttons to recognize:

1) Words and Phrases

Sit down and think for a moment. What are some things that colleagues and employees say that rub you the wrong way? Are there particular words or phras-es that irk you or are "hot-buttons" for your temper? Of course there are, and it's important to realize them. For example, "absolute" phrases get to me. If someone says, "Jermaine, you *never* take out the trash," I immediately want to respond with a defensive response like, "I *never*? I *never* take out the trash?"

Now, I am known for my huge smile, positive outlook on life, and mildly upbeat persona; however, there are times when I have a bad day, and during those days, I am more likely to behave in a quiet, reserved, and introspective manner. I can feel myself leaving my base-line when individuals don't respect the fact that it's just "one of those days." So, if people ask me if I'm crabby repeatedly, well, that makes me crabby! Sometimes when people persist that I'm acting crabby due to my silence or quiet behavior (although I've explained to them that it's just one of those days), I become even crabbier when they don't respect my personal space and previous response. I am aware of this question as an emotional trigger and hot-button for me, so when someone comes up to me and asks repeatedly if I'm crabby, I make the per-son aware of how that question affects me or once again I go out of my way to explain that it's just one of those days today. And, of course, I pray that they get the message.

2) Behaviors and Mannerisms

There are also non-verbal triggers which include how individuals communicate and send messages through body language such as posture, gestures, and facial expressions. For example, someone's trigger can be having a listener roll her or his eyes or sigh in a show of boredom, discontent, or disagreement. Behavioral triggers include the act of interruption or the use of sarcasm and shutting out, such as someone saying, "Talk to the hand." These can be done by anyone, including colleagues, employees, friends, family members, and strangers alike, and they all can have the same negative affect on you.

3) Personality Types

Have you ever met or worked with a colleague or leader who was argumentative, chronically indecisive, cynical, impatient, intolerant of others' differences, narcissistic, overbearing, overly critical, rigid in their thinking or self-righteous? If you have, I can guestimate that one of these personality types ignited your emotional or mental triggers. Keep in mind that what triggers one person's hot-buttons may only generate a smile or frown for someone else. There are certain personality types that can annoy, frustrate, or anger you enough to cause you to leave your base-line or normal emotional state in an instant. A "yes" woman or man, a "no" woman or man, or someone who won't pick a side could each be an emotional trigger or hot-button for you.

4) Specific People

Who could you name that, even if you just *see* them, will set off your emotional triggers and cause you to leave your base-line? Could this be an ex-girlfriend or ex-boyfriend, a friend who betrayed you, a lazy employee, a deceptive colleague, an arrogant leader, or just someone who you simply don't like? This person can just push all your buttons the wrong way. You might still have to deal with specific people, regardless of whether they are a trigger for you. Remember in the workplace you still have a professional obligation to do the right thing even when you strongly dislike the individual.

If you struggle with how to identify your triggers, I have outlined in the following table a collection of examples to review.

Workshop Participants Share Examples of "Emotional Triggers" and "Hot-Buttons"

Words and Phrases	Behaviors and Mannerisms	Personality Types
• We've always done it this way. • That's the company culture around here. • Never. • I can't. • That's stupid. • You can't do that; that's impossible to do. • Come on, now. • No! (without consideration). • Corporate buzz-words (in general). • It's the company policy! • We need to talk. • Do you have a moment or I need to talk with you (makes me feel like I'm about to be punished). • Any use of profanity. • Any racist, sexist, or homophobic jokes. • That's not true.	• Lazy people. • Getting up and writing on the dry-erase board during meetings while others are talking. • Coming late to meetings. • Not having an agenda prior to a team meeting. • Not explaining the purpose of a team meeting. • Treating every problem as an emergency that must be handled immediately. • Crossing and folding arms defensively. • Looking at you over her or his glasses with head down. • Looking at cell phones to see who called during a meeting. • Typing on laptops during meetings. • Text messaging while talking to someone.	• Know-it-alls. • Sarcastic people. • Indecisive people. • People who try to talk over you. • Redundant communicators. • People who always apologize. • People who are calm no matter what's going on. • People who act busy so no one bothers them. • Drama queens and kings. • Close-minded leaders and colleagues. • Impatient people. • Leaders and colleagues who always have to be right. • Conversation monopolizers. • Controlling leaders and colleagues. • Energy drainers (negative and pessimistic people).

Body Talk—Can You Hear Your Body Communicating with You?

When you move away from your base-line, you always get a fair warning from your body. *Body talk is when your body communicates with you emotionally, mentally, non-verbally, and physiologically before you leave your base-line.* We are always given a status update before we become emotionally explosive or before we simply "snap" on leaders, colleagues, and employees. Body talk alerts us before, during, and after emotional reactions and outbursts. The question then becomes are you listening and considering *your* body talk? *The technical terminology for body talk is "proprioceptive stimuli." Propriceptive stimuli are the internal and physiological changes a person experiences while having strong and intense emotions.* Adler, Proctor, and Towne write, "For example, the physical components of fear include an increased heart rate, a rise in blood pressure, an increase in adrenaline secretions, an elevated blood sugar level, a slowing of digestion, and a dilation of pupils. A churning stomach or tense jaw can be a signal that something is wrong." Oftentimes, people ignore their body talk because they simply don't realize or aren't listening to the fact that it's talking to them. Other times, people ignore the warning signs. Either way, the person is not utilizing emotional intelligence and is moving into potentially dangerous waters as she or he leaves her or his base-line. When leaders and employees disregard or disobey their body talk, they usually move from professional behaviors to unprofessional behaviors. And, we all know unprofessionalism can lead to costly lawsuits and unfortunate terminations. Your body communicates with you on three levels—*physical, mental, and emotional*—before you leave your base-line.

1) **Physical body talk** can include becoming shaky, grinding your teeth, clenching your fist, biting your bottom lip, cracking your knuckles, clicking your pen nervously, biting your nails, playing with your hair, getting a tick, fidgeting, or feeling cold or hot. Poker players might call these characteristics "tells." These are indicators that you are leaving your base-line when you can actually see or feel changes taking place inside your body. Remember Dr. Albert Mehrabian's research that "93% of all communication is non-verbal." Observers of colleagues, employees, and leaders can get a good idea of their emotional state by watching these non-verbal reactions and responses.

2) **Mental hints** that you are moving away from your base-line might be that your thought process is functioning differently. You feel more disorganized, or all of a sudden you are hit by unmanageable thoughts. Thinking negatively when you are normally a positive person and thinking irrationally when you are normally rational are also cues that you are functioning outside of your normal mode.

3) **Emotional signs** are based on how you *feel*. Hopelessness, helplessness, fury, excitement, or "out of control" are feelings often associated with being moved away from one's base-line. Emotional indications are often confused with mental ones because they are so closely related. However, it's not as important to differentiate which way your body is communicating to you as it is to realize simply that your body is talking to you and telling you that you are moving into a danger zone.

Body Talk Indicators

Physical Signs and Symptoms	Mental Signs and Symptoms	Emotional Signs and Symptoms
Shaky	Disorganized	Feelings of Hopelessness
Grinding your teeth	Thinking negatively	Feelings of Helplessness
Clenching your fist	Thinking irrationally	Fury
Biting your bottom lip	Violent thoughts	Excitement
Cracking your knuckles	Vindictive thoughts	Out of control
Clicking your pen nervously	A lose-lose paradigm	Fear
Biting your nails	A win-lose paradigm	Aggression
Playing with your hair	Jealous thoughts	Rage
Getting a tick	Destructive thoughts	Negative Anger
Fidgeting	Pessimistic thinking	Constant Anxiety
Feeling cold or hot	Selfish thinking	Agitation/Irritation
Pacing back and forth		
Pounding on objects		

THE FOUR COMMUNICATION STYLES

When seeking to communicate appropriately, competently, and effectively, it is important to also be aware of the four communication styles. The inability to understand these four styles or using them at the wrong times can lead to conflict or inhibit open and honest communication. Let's take a look at the four styles of communication, how they function, and how you can work to enhance and promote clear communication.

Passive Style

A passive communicator is unwilling or unable to express beliefs, emotions, and needs. This communicator is "hard to read" and can be frustrating to work with because she or he acts like a blank wall in communication situations. Why are passive communicators hard to read? Passive communicators don't address or deal with problems directly; they escape their personal and professional issues through apathy, avoidance, denial, minimization, tuning-out, and withdrawal. Dr. Albert Ellis describes passive communicators in *How to Control Your Anger Before It Controls You* when he writes, "You want something and do not honestly express your want or make any real effort to obtain it. You resort to indirect, passive, somewhat dishonest actions. You frequently do not admit to yourself what you really want and don't want. You needlessly inhibit yourself and even deny some of your basic desires. You tend to feel anxious, hurt, and angry."

Common Attitudes and Behaviors of Passive Communicators	Strategies for Communicating with Passive Communicators
• Lack the courage to stand up for themselves. • Avoid chaos, conflict, and challenging situations at all costs. • Agree to commit to things they really don't want to do. • Say yes when they really mean no. • Are overly agreeable and rarely express their true beliefs, emotions, and needs. • Tend to sound apprehensive, hesitant, and unsure. • Don't make eye contact and do not appear confident. • Speak in low or soft voices and come across as soft, weak, and meek. • Appear to be victims by sounding helpless and hopeless.	• Create a safe work environment for communication and participation to take place. • Encourage them to communicate and participate. • Teach and show them how to communicate and participate effectively. • Don't attack, retaliate, or punish them for having an opposing viewpoint when they finally do take the risk to communicate and participate. • Avoid responding defensively.

Aggressive Style

An aggressive communicator expresses her or his beliefs, emotions, and needs in a hostile, intimidating, and controlling manner. Autocratic leaders tend to communicate this way. Historically, aggression means "to attack," which confirms the normal engagement style of an aggressive communicator. Rather than simply being enthusiastic about the subject, they communicate negativity and express undertones that can feel threatening and unpleasant. Dr. Albert Ellis states that as aggressive communicators, "You feel angry towards others for blocking your goals and often try to do them in rather than to get what you want. You are emotionally honest but in an inappropriate way. You behave actively and assertively but at the expense of others. You express yourself fully— and frequently overdo it. You often feel self righteous and superior to others and tend to damn them."

© 1999 Ted Goff

"The next time something's about to go wrong, I want one of you losers to speak up."

Common Attitudes and Behaviors of Aggressive Communicators	Strategies for Communicating with Aggressive Communicators
• Need to win and maintain control, regardless of the method they use. • Will go to any length to control and take over an argument or discussion. • Turn friendly discussions into fights, and are driven to win at any cost. • Display aggressive body language such as finger pointing, invading personal and professional space, pounding tables, screaming, and yelling. • Use insults, manipulation, and profanity to control situations and people. • Stare others down with piercing, intimidating looks. • Command, demand, and bark orders rather than asking politely, respectfully, and professionally. • Are cynical and find fault with others and their ideas.	• Capture the individual's attention in a respectful and non-aggressive manner (If known, call them by name or a properly respective address or title, i.e. "Sir," "Ma'am," "Officer," "Your Honor"). • Seek immediately to reduce any aggression or tension. • Tactfully take a stand, and don't back down while communicating your beliefs, emotions, and needs (choose your battles wisely). • Appropriately interrupt the aggressor when necessary (inappropriate interruptions can lead to verbal, emotional and/or physical aggression).

Passive-Aggressive Style

A passive-aggressive communicator expresses beliefs, emotions, and needs in an ambiguous, indirect, and unclear manner. They use sarcasm whenever possible, and the true nature of what they are thinking or feeling is intentionally left unclear. They attempt to operate in the best of both worlds, but they often create more problems and headaches for themselves and for those who work with them regularly. Passive-aggressive communicators have also been labeled "dirty fighters" and "crazy-makers" because of their selfishness, unfairness, and indirectness when dealing with conflict and communication challenges. The authors of *Looking Out, Looking In* explain crazy making when they write, "It occurs when people have feelings of resentment, anger, or rage that they are unable or unwilling to express directly. Instead of keeping these feelings to themselves, a crazymaker sends aggressive messages in subtle, indirect ways, thus maintaining the front of kindness. This amiable facade eventually crumbles, however, leaving the crazymaker's victim confused and angry at having been fooled."

© 1996 Ted Goff

"See? That means, 'What do you clowns want?"

Common Attitudes and Behaviors of Passive-Aggressive Communicators	Strategies for Communicating with Passive-Aggressive Communicators
• Externally appear to agree with you but internally do not and thus are deceptive—consciously or otherwise. • Send mixed messages because their words contradict their behaviors. • Avoid verbal commitments, avoid committing to tasks, play semantic games, beat around the bush, and waste others' time. • Communicate with undertones, such as cutting remarks, sarcasm, and subtle digs. • Use misinterpretation and misunderstanding as excuses to avoid responsibility. • Refuse to speak up to resolve conflict when they have the opportunity and would rather gossip and criticize others and their ideas. • Will not confront the source of a disagreement directly — indirectly complain about the source behind her or his backs and behind closed doors. • Roll eyes during disagreements, make disturbing "sighing" noises, shake their heads inappropriately, and smile and smirk when others oppose their perspective or position.	• Communicate openly, honestly, and truthfully with them. • Create a safe environment for them to communicate openly, honestly, and truthfully with you. • Avoid responding defensively. • Do not retaliate or become aggressive when they are open, honest, and truthful with you about how they feel. • Be crystal clear about what you need, want, or expect of them. • Secure a commitment, hold them accountable, and follow up with them.

Assertive Style

An assertive communicator expresses her or his beliefs, emotions, and needs respectfully and encourages others to do the same. An assertive communicator wants to honor the communication process by creating a healthy exchange of ideas and emotions so that everyone is heard, respected, and valued when expressing what matters most to them. The members of a tight team of assertive communicators operate generally in synergy with one another, which creates cohesion, unity, and harmony in the workplace. Ellis states that as an assertive communicator, "You want something, and honestly acknowledge to yourself that you want it. You tend to act openly with others. You respect other peoples' values and goals but often prefer your own to theirs. You behave actively and expressively."

Common Attitudes and Behaviors of Assertive Communicators	Strategies for Communicating with Assertive Communicators
• Show sincerity and respect when communicating with others. • Seek first to understand, then to be understood. • Postpone judgment when listening to others and don't interrupt when others are talking. • Communicate honestly, openly, and truthfully with others. • Create a safe, healthy, and friendly environment in which others can communicate honestly, openly, and truthfully. • Monitor personal behaviors when communicating with others and adjust communication style when necessary. • Don't avoid conflict, rather address and deal with conflict willingly, effectively, and proactively. • Don't play games, beat around the bush, or waste others' time when communicating with them. • Maintain professionalism even when there are apparent personality clashes, communication challenges, and professional conflicts. • Apologize and own their behaviors when they offend others.	• Communicate openly, honestly, and truthfully with them. • Prepare to have a mutual exchange of personal and professional ideas. • Be prepared to be asked clarifying questions by them and to paraphrase or offer an example of the assertive communicator's ideas for clarification purposes. • Respect the fact that they have the right to an opposing viewpoint and the freedom to disagree with you; don't take conflict personally. • Be crystal clear about what you need, want, or expect from them.

Real-World Challenge: On your team, there is one member who talks incessantly. Some of her or his ideas are good, but generally, she or he just complains or brings up issues not on the agenda. How and where do you attend to this problem?

WHICH COMMUNICATION STYLE IS THE BEST?

Whether I'm presenting this body of research in a classroom or at a conference, everyone wants to know which style is the most effective or if she or he has to abandon one style and adopt another style to be a relationship-based leader. Many theorists, authors, scholars, and lay people argue fiercely that the assertive style is without a doubt the best of all four. Others believe the best communication occurs when a communicator uses a combination of all four communication styles. Too much of any one style can be overdone; eventually, too much of one style can have an adverse effect.

I believe the best communicators are those who have a variety of tools in their communication toolbox because every communication encounter requires a different tool to succeed. Renowned psychologist Abraham Maslow says it best, "If the only tool in your toolbox is a hammer you'll treat everything [communication problem or conflict] as a nail." Those who lead with greatness add new tools constantly to their leadership and communication toolboxes. A relationship-based leader must use the communication style most fitting to her or his environment. Competent communicators and relationship-based leaders understand that they will, at times, have to make changes and adjustments to accomplish communication and leadership goals. They will need to fluctuate and switch tools as they interact with diverse ideas, people, personalities, work styles, and workplace environments.

These variables will greatly affect how you communicate with others and will help you to determine which communication style will reap the greatest benefits and rewards. Being too passive, aggressive, passive-aggressive, or assertive can work against you when used inappropriately or at inopportune times. I strongly favor developing assertiveness skills for life, school, and work, but I also understand that balance and moderation are critical in all things. My final suggestion is to size up your communication environment and situation every single time to discern which style is most appropriate and effective, and read the next section to understand how applying this information to conflict resolution is essential to creating workplace harmony.

Knowing Which Communication Style Fits Best

We were having our end-of-the-semester faculty meeting, and one of my colleagues began to attack me in front of my colleagues and peers. Now, I would normally describe my communication style as assertive, and if I'm not being emotionally intelligent, I can leave my base-line and move from being assertive to being aggressive. In this particular meeting, I allowed my colleague to attack me continuously without responding verbally. Several of my colleagues and teaching peers were bewildered that I didn't assert myself even once during the meeting. After the meeting, someone said to me, "Jermaine, how could you allow that person to disrespect you in front of the entire Humanities faculty?" Another colleague said, "I'm not sure if I should honor and applaud you or if I should be disappointed with you."

Even if no one else knew why I wasn't responding verbally to the aggressive attacks, I certainly knew. I did not respond because, prior to the meeting, I had had a *huge* argument with my uncle, Michael; I was full of mixed emotions and psychological noise which was ready to manifest itself through anger, frustration, fear, and vindictiveness. I knew my emotional and mental threshold going into the meeting. Honestly, I knew that the best communication style to use during that particular meeting was to be passive because I was not physically, emotionally, mentally, or spiritually equipped to deal constructively with conflict that particular day. I was on *edge*—multiplied by a hundred—so I had to adjust my communication style appropriately and accordingly.

PART SIX

Handling and Resolving Conflict as a Leader

Do I Have to Deal with Conflict?

Conflict, hate it or love it, is here to stay, and as long as we are breathing fresh or polluted air, we will all encounter and experience conflict as we communicate and interact with others. You may even know people who *love* to argue and debate. In the article, "How to Turn Debate into Dialogues," best-selling author of *You Just Don't Understand*, Deborah Tannen, Ph.D. says that, "As Americans we live in an argument culture, where opposition, debate, polarization, litigation, attacks, and criticism are perceived as the best way to get anything done." You may know people who embrace conflict graciously; you may know others who are conflict-challenged and cringe at the very thought of dealing with conflict. For the latter, I say you may run, run, run, but you can't hide, hide, hide from the reality of conflict. Relationship-based leaders who lead with greatness cannot afford to be allergic to conflict. They cannot be conflict-challenged or have a significant aversion towards conflict. I'm not saying leaders have to love conflict, but I am suggesting that relationship-based leaders become more acquainted, familiar, skilled, and comfortable with handling workplace disagreements and team conflict. I've encountered highly intelligent and savvy leaders who have run in the opposite direction when certain departments were colliding or certain individuals were having differences of opinion within the organization; avoiding conflict only leads to more team problems and a leader's loss of credibility.

You have probably heard many times that conflict is natural, and I hope you would agree because it is. The fact that we all have different beliefs, perceptions, views, ethics, morals, and values tells me that a conflict is usually standing right next to us in the workplace. The etymology of the word "conflict" means "to strike or to strike against." When colleagues and employees believe or feel their beliefs, perceptions, views, ethics, morals, and values are being disregarded, disrespected, or minimized, they tend to strike out at leaders and colleagues to settle the score or "to get even." According to the *Random House College Dictionary*, the word *"strike" means to deal a blow or strike to, as with the fist, a weapon, or a hammer.* Data and research show that workplace violence is increasing. We've read the newspaper headlines and seen the gruesome stories on television of people striking back with physical violence when they feel their needs, wants, or expectations are not being met or are being violated. Yet, while employees may use physical aggression to strike out against colleagues or leaders, such explosions are not the norm. Most employees strike out passively or passive-aggressively in subtle ways to destroy and erode organizational progress and achievements. Unhappy and dissatisfied colleagues and employees usually punish their leaders in organizations by refusing to be effective, efficient, and productive employees. These types of employees can cause a team to collapse or an organization to go bankrupt. Relationship-based leaders must deal effectively with this conflict before it spreads throughout the organization like a cancer or an uncontrollable forest fire. Don't shy away from conflict; instead, welcome the conflict as a way to get the real issues out on the table for team discussion. A healthy team discussion regarding team conflict reduces stress because it alleviates tension. My zillion-dollar secret to resolving conflict is to *learn* and *understand* why employees strike out in the first place. Unfortunately, most leaders get emotionally caught up and swept away in the conflict without figuring out what caused the conflict, so they struggle to resolve the matter.

Here's another one of my zillion-dollar secrets: *All conflict is the result of an unmet or violated need, want, or expectation.* That's it—plain and simple! People strike out against others personally and professionally when they are not getting their needs, wants, and expectations met and satisfied. Now, a relationship-based leader can't always meet every need, want, and expectation of their colleagues and employees, but understanding *why* they are striking out puts you in a position to have meaningful dialogue. Dealing with conflict isn't easy, but relationship-based leaders must develop effective conflict resolution skills. Conflict denial is a fatal flaw of any leader.

Is Conflict Constructive or Destructive, Good or Bad, Positive or Negative?

It's none of the above—or all of the above! Conflict is only what you make of it. So, conflict can be constructive or destructive, good or bad, and positive or negative. My question to leaders is, "How comfortable are you with handling conflict when it takes place in your organization?" I once asked 500 corporate

© 2001 Ted Goff

"I'd like to remind everyone that there will be no pie throwing during this meeting."

directors and senior level executives during a conference, "When conflict arises, are you a conflict optimist or a conflict pessimist?" About one-third of the leaders identified as conflict pessimists for one or more reasons: (1) inability to deal with conflict effectively; (2) fear of mishandling the conflict; and/or (3) perceived conflict as emotionally draining, so conflict is avoided altogether. Conflict can be handled appropriately or inappropriately, but this is solely determined by the leaders' attitudes and dispositions. What is your attitude and disposition towards conflict? Is it constructive or destructive, optimistic or pessimistic, good or bad, or positive or negative?

CONSTRUCTIVE CONFLICT

Constructive conflict occurs when team members can comfortably and safely express their points of disagreements in a healthy work environment without fear of retaliation and negative pushback. The ultimate goal of constructive conflict is to move the organization forward by accomplishing its purpose, vision, and goals. Constructive conflict and high trust teams can make better decisions and increase team performance. Why? Team members simply feel respected, safe, valued, and listened-to as colleagues and employees of the organization. Organizations and teams who can argue and debate difficult issues honestly, openly, and respectfully with one another tend to increase team trust and build stronger relationships and powerful organizations.

Constructive Conflict

- Helps the team and organization move forward successfully.

- Builds and increases team trust.

- Confronts and deals with team conflict appropriately.

- Welcomes and respects colleagues' and employees' opinions.

- Team communication is honest, open, and respectful.

- Focuses on communication and cooperation (solution-based thinking).

- Colleagues' and employees' needs, wants, and expectations are addressed and met if possible.

DESTRUCTIVE CONFLICT

Destructive conflict occurs when team members feel uncomfortable and fearful of expressing their points of disagreement due to an unhealthy work environment of low trust and disrespectful leaders and colleagues. This work environment

© 2002 Ted Goff

"Who wants to tell Mr. Carton
that the foyer is on fire?"

usually breeds negative behaviors and feelings of aggression, hostility, resentment, stubbornness, and vindictiveness. Destructive conflict is detrimental to the organization's purpose, vision, and goals because teams are less likely to complete tasks and projects on time. Of course, this result jeopardizes the organization's profits, as well as potential and current business relationships with customers, clients, and shareholders. If a relationship-based leader doesn't take action swiftly, destructive conflict has the potential to permanently destroy team morale, as well as organizational success and achievements.

> **Destructive Conflict**
>
> • Prevents the team and organization from moving forward successfully.
>
> • Lowers or destroys team trust, motivation, and morale.
>
> • Avoids, denies, or minimizes organizational conflict.
>
> • Apathetic towards colleagues' and employees' opinions.
>
> • Team communication is ambiguous, indirect, and unclear.
>
> • Focuses on chaos and conflict (problem-based thinking).
>
> • Colleagues' and employees' needs, wants, or expectations are not addressed or rarely met.

The 3 Nasty Evils of Destructive Conflict

We have already defined and discussed the negative effects of destructive conflict on teams and organizations, but how does it affect leaders? Some leaders, whether they have been victims of destructive conflict or simply have never learned to deal with conflict, resort to negative habits that only worsen the situation. These habits typically unveil themselves in one of three ways and which almost always causes harm to personal, professional, and intimate relationships. It is important for relationship-based leaders to be aware of how destructive conflict infiltrates their behaviors when they are fearful of confronting difficult team and organizational issues.

If a leader isn't comfortable, competent, or confident when handling conflict, she or he will most likely deal with the conflict in one or all of the three destructive ways: *(1) conflict avoidance*, whereby an individual ignores differences emotionally, mentally, and/or physically; *(2) conflict denial*, whereby an individual deliberately refuses to acknowledge, admit, or recognize the fact that disagreements or differences exist; and *(3) conflict minimization*, whereby an individual, through manipulative communication, seeks to reduce the disagreement's significance.

Conflict Avoidance

The original meaning of "avoid" in Latin is "to empty" and "to remove the contents." Leaders who avoid conflict attempt essentially to remove any and all conflict from their presence; they simply want to eliminate the conflict through physical, emotional, and mental avoidance. Conflict-avoidant leaders are quite aware of the conflict that exists in their organizations, but they ignore it rather than deal with it constructively. By deliberately choosing not to address, confront, and deal with conflict, such leaders deteriorate team morale and inhibit organizational growth. When leaders avoid conflict, they increase everyone's stress level; chronic and untreated stress eventually leads to individual and organizational burnout. Burnout, of course, destroys and kills personal motivation and innovation that organizations desperately need in order to be economically-successful. When leaders avoid conflict, they actually obstruct organizational recovery.

© 2001 Ted Goff

"We've decided to devote more people to ignoring the problem to make it go away faster."

Those who avoid conflict are more focused on their personal apprehensions, fears, and hang-ups rather than on the overall good of the organization. What do you think colleagues and employees say about leaders who are conflict avoidant? Would you call them courageous or cowardly leaders? Can conflict avoidant leaders build credibility and trust? Can they motivate, inspire, and influence team members when they lack the courage to confront conflict? You decide!

Conflict Denial

In its Latin root, the meaning of "denial" is "to say no." Leaders who deny conflict convey to their colleagues and employees, "Conflict doesn't exist around here." They deliberately refuse to acknowledge, admit, or recognize the presence of team and organization conflict. They even refuse to acknowledge its existence in the face of substantial evidence from respected colleagues and employees. How would you feel, as a colleague or employee, if a leader denied and rejected the valid evidence you presented to her or him? Would you or could you follow a leader in conflict denial?

The conflict avoidant leader is at least cognizant of the conflict but chooses not to do anything about it. The conflict denial leader fights against and refuses to accept the fact that conflict exists. A leader in denial of conflict can *never* grow and develop an organization to its fullest and maximum potential. If an organization has an unhealthy work culture due to unresolved conflict, the conflict denial leader will never be able to change that culture until she or he acknowledges and admits that conflict exists. Colleagues and employees will *never* commit and dedicate themselves 100% to a leader who denies, denounces, refuses, and rejects their valid concerns regarding team or organizational conflict.

Relationship-based leadership is all about listening to what matters most to your colleagues and employees. I love it when Dr. Phil says, "You cannot change what you do not acknowledge." Leaders cannot change the atmosphere, climate, culture, feel, mood, or direction of a team or organization if she or he isn't courageous and humble enough to deal with reality. Why do leaders deny and reject the realities of conflict when colleagues and employees have clearly identified the conflict for them? How much does conflict denial cost a leader and organization on a daily basis?

Conflict Minimization

Have you ever been disrespected by a leader within your organization? If you've worked with a leader who minimizes conflict, controversial issues, and difficult dialogues, I know you've been disrespected. *Conflict minimization occurs when a leader reduces conflict to the smallest size possible.* Their goal is to make the conflict as insignificant and unimportant as possible in your mind and in their own. These leaders believe that if they can convince you that your issue is small, insignificant, or unimportant, there will be no expectation from you for them to take immediate action to resolve the conflict. Conflict minimizers are skilled at convincing colleagues and employees to perceive their conflict concerns as miniscule issues. Through manipulative communication, conflict minimizing leaders down-play conflict by saying things like, "Just let it blow over," "It's no big deal," "Don't stress yourself out over a small matter," "Just let it go," or "Trust me on this one; it will work itself out." *Conflict minimization is a defense mechanism used to reduce the leader's anxiety, fear, and stress because she or he perceives conflict as too overwhelming to address, confront, or deal with directly.*

PREPARING TO DEAL WITH CONFLICT

As a relationship-based leader, you need to know that conflict is inevitable in the workplace and among your team members. When conflict is not dealt with properly, it festers, creates bad emotions, gets blown out of proportion, and encourages gossip and destructive rumors. How you handle conflict will be carefully scrutinized by many. Relationship-based leaders know conflict can't be avoided, denied, or minimized. Therefore, it makes sense for you to think in advance about how you plan to approach conflict when it arises. The following five points will help you deal with conflict more appropriately when you face a challenging situation. These points will also come in handy when you are selecting the best communication style to use to resolve conflict among colleagues and employees.

Know Thyself

This means having an acute awareness of who you are as a communicator and as a leader. What are your T.A.G.S.? What are your areas that need most improvement? What are your emotional thresholds? What kinds of things trigger you to engage in less-than-exemplary behaviors? How will you know when you are in over your head? What is your body talk saying to you? It doesn't take a therapist to answer these questions; careful self-examination suffices. Approaching a conflict situation requires that you ask yourself, "Should I confront and deal with a difficult dialogue at this time, and is this the most appropriate place to deal with this conflict?" If it isn't the right time or place, wait, but remember not to ignore it altogether. Waiting may mean that the end result leads to a much better resolution for everyone. On the other hand, not being aware of your mental, emotional, and physical state when dealing with conflict practically guarantees you'll find yourself in a personal or professional mess.

Remember the story I told at the end of last section? I was in the semester-end faculty meeting, and I chose passive communication rather than assertive communication because I knew that I would become aggressive. I knew *myself* that day because I checked my emotional temperature before entering the meeting and my temperature read "explosive." I was on the verge of an emotional eruption, like an uncontrollable volcano. I can honestly say I now understand what the phrase "You have to learn how to pick and choose your battles" means. I am happy I chose wisely! What would you have done?

Know Thy Goals

In conflict, every person desperately tries to achieve her or his personal or professional goals. Having a clear understanding of what you are trying to achieve during conflict will determine how you treat others. As you pursue your goals, ask yourself, "Do you want to create a positive or negative experience for yourself and others?" Approach your team interactions with specific goals, and have a plan in mind as to how to achieve them. Share those goals with your team. When everyone knows the game plan, goal-related conflict is less likely to arise. Ask yourself if the goals are fair, realistic, and reasonable. Are they inclusive of the other person or team members? Preparing yourself to enter into possible conflict in this manner shows your colleagues and employees that you respect them even if you don't agree with them.

> ### *You Don't Get What You Want—You Get What You Expect!*
>
> Prior to dealing with and confronting conflict, you should always know what you expect to accomplish. Ask yourself, "What do I expect to achieve as a result of talking with colleagues or employees? What would I like to have happen or what would I like to see changed as a result of being assertive?" When relationship-based leaders experience difficult workplace issues, the goal is to move from workplace *difficulty* to workplace *ease*. The problem is that most people whine, complain, and want to feel better but haven't taken the time to think about what "better" looks like or feels like.

As a relationship-based leader, you must be able to clearly articulate what you need, want, and expect before someone can attempt to give it to you. Most people just want you to make them feel better. Unfortunately, there is one step you must take before you can feel better: identify your desired outcomes. Your goals will determine which communication style you use and how you treat the person while interacting with them. Your goals are created by your motives and intentions, which are responsible for guiding your behavior. If your goal is to win the argument, you will more than likely disregard having a professional and personal relationship with a colleague. I believe the French playwright Albert Camus said it best, "The need to be right—the sign of a vulgar mind." If you have a *need* to win an argument and to be *right*, it's safe to say that you don't care very much about relationship building because winning at all costs means you may fight dirty and unfairly by not listening or by ignoring your colleagues' and employees' ideas and perspectives. Conversely, if your goal is to create a *win-win* relationship with a colleague or employee, you will maintain a level of professionalism and respect for that colleague. Although you might be having heated exchanges over the conflict, your goal is to keep the win-win philosophy in mind during the conflict.

Know the Other Person(s)

Are your colleagues and employees serious individuals? Does your leader follow the letter of the law or the law's spirit when she or he leads? Are your team members abrasive and abrupt when they communicate, or are they relaxed and easy-going? This is when it's really helpful to have done your homework and to know your colleagues' and employees' T.A.G.S. before conflict occurs. This is also where using the D.A.L.O. Approach and your "leadership by walking around" will really pay off. Is this a colleague, employee, or leader with whom you would normally laugh and joke? Is this a defensive colleague, or a fairly open-minded one? Strategies that work for some colleagues will not work for others. The more you communicate with colleagues and employees, the more you begin to understand them. The more you understand a person, the more you are able to communicate effectively with her or him. That's why it's so important to take into account people's personalities, work styles, and idiosyncrasies when you try to communicate with them. As a relationship-based leader, you should understand your colleagues and employees in a way that makes conflict resolution more effective and palatable.

Know the Communication Context

Another one of my favorite quotations says, "You must know the waters in which you swim." Knowing the communication context in which you are functioning means you understand and know the situation, setting, mood, or temperature of the communication environment. Effective communication cannot take place if you are not aware of the variables that make up the context in which you find yourself. Relationship-based leaders should know the waters in which they are leading and communicating if they really want to make a difference. This means doing your homework with due diligence before you attempt to reach and lead the people within the organization. Remember: relationship-based leadership occurs when a leader deliberately establishes and builds an interpersonal relationship with their colleagues and employees before attempting to lead them. Find out what you are up against and what potential dangers may await you. No, you won't uncover every challenging problem, and you will have a multitude of surprises (because surprises come with the leadership position), but you *do* want to know the waters in which you are swimming. I try to know the waters in which I swim before I deliver a presentation at a conference or organization because I want to know what lies ahead of me. I simply use a pre-engagement questionnaire and speak with several people to gather as much information as possible regarding the psychology of the conference participants. Knowing the context of a conference allows me to tailor my presentations to a formal or casual audience. I need to know whether I am speaking with students or with business professionals. Knowing the waters I'll be swimming in helps me pick the best examples to share so I can convey my points effectively. I can't even begin to tell you how many speeches and workshops I would have bombed and butchered had I not done my homework with due diligence.

When working in a team, there is a time and a place for everything. You may be perfectly ready to begin furthering your goals without recognizing that your team has completely different perceptions of what you should be doing. When you're on one page and they're on another, conflict and stress is inevitable. When conflict arises, you need to understand when and where to stage your battles and when to leave them alone. A basic rule of thumb is to praise in public and criticize in private. This point is crucial. Conflict that arises in a room full of colleagues and employees may wound another person's ego and embarrass them. Conflict matters dealt with in private are much more likely to be resolved because you honor their personal and professional pride and dignity. Remember the mantra of Mary Kay Ash of Mary Kay Cosmetics, "Make Me Feel Important."

Know the Best and Most Appropriate Communication Style

This process involves a bit of human psychology, practice, and finesse—and knowing the different communication styles and how to deal effectively with each of them. If leading colleagues and employees is a new task for you, it may be impossible to guess what will work and what won't work when dealing with conflict among different work styles, personality types, and communication styles. Remember the four communication styles (passive, aggressive, passive-aggressive, and assertive) and learn which style will work best for the environment where you are leading. I suggest using the strategies I've provided to increase your probability of a successful communication interaction. Be aware of your style and practice the most appropriate communication style when necessary.

This practice is called communication flexibility, not hypocrisy or double-mindedness; remember that your goal is to be an *effective* communicator and relationship-based leader. Interestingly, being an assertive communicator (usually the ideal style) may not work with very passive individuals. Assertive communicators have a high propensity to (unintentionally) intimidate passive communicators who may secretly feel insecure, ill-equipped, and incompetent around highly competent and confident communicators. The passive communicator may refuse to get involved in a conflict that requires extended dialogue and professional vulnerability. She or he is most likely expecting leadership and guidance from you and not a conversation or democratic dialogue. That's why it's important that your goals include some benefit for the other person to motivate them to get involved and participate.

Leaders have to be clear and specific about the practical benefits colleagues and employees will gain by supporting the leaders' efforts and initiatives. This is called the Social Gain Theory. *The Social Gain Theory contends that when colleagues and employees do a favor for you, they want to know how you will return the favor to them.* In other words, "What kind of benefits will I personally or professionally gain from helping you?" When I worked in marketing and sales for several snack food companies, the marketing and sales managers always taught us one simple rule of selling: the W.I.I.F.M. Theory, which translates into "What's In It For Me?" They said, "If you can show grocery store owners, store managers, and decision-makers *what's in it for them*, you increase your probability of making the sale." As a relationship-based leader, ask yourself how you can use the W.I.I.F.M. Theory to help you motivate and lead your colleagues and employees to greatness.

WHAT'S ALL THE FUSS ABOUT? (TYPES OF CONFLICT)

Earlier, I shared my zillion-dollar secret to resolving personal, professional, and intimate conflict, which entails fully understanding that all conflict is the result of an unmet or violated need, want or expectation. Always keep this zillion-dollar secret in mind because it is highly essential to resolving all conflicts.

A valuable tool in resolving conflict is understanding what the conflict is all about and what caused the conflict. Leaders must be able to identify workplace conflicts before they can resolve the conflict. Three types of conflict can plague and destroy cohesive teamwork and threaten a company's growth and potential success: (1) substantive conflict; (2) procedural conflict; and/or (3) interpersonal conflict. It is important for a relationship-based leader to be able to precisely diagnose which kind of conflict is plaguing her or his organization before attempting to resolve the conflict. Simply knowing the three types of conflict you are dealing with goes a long way toward conflict resolution.

Substantive Conflict

Substantive conflict involves a conflict between ideas and issues. In a team setting, team members often disagree over the merits of ideas, projects, priorities, work assignments, organizational direction, and team goals. Your leadership in resolving these matters is crucial. Every team member deserves to know, early in the process, your perspective and your expectations of the team's goals. Priorities can be set collectively with the understanding that your role as a relationship-based leader carries more weight in these decisions when necessary. This doesn't mean that you are choosing to be an autocratic leader; rather, you want your team to know that you might have to carry the deciding vote—especially during crisis, conflict, and important deadlines.

Imagine, for example, that your organization has started a new "healthy lifestyles" initiative for a better workplace, and your team has been asked to provide ideas as to which programs will inaugurate the initiative. Ideas flow from your team members, such as a daycare center, pet daycare, flexible work hours, and job sharing. These are all good ideas, but the company has allocated money for only one of these for the upcoming year. Everyone will have an opinion, and there is potential for the team to become chaotic and divided. As a relationship-based leader, it is your job to carefully decide the most viable choice for implementation, to dialogue with the team, and to get the backing of your colleagues and employees by the end of the task.

Procedural Conflict

Procedural conflict—also known as process conflict—occurs when team members collide over the best strategies for implementing the ideas upon which the team has collectively agreed. While they agree on ideas, they differ on the *how*—the steps they need to actualize the goals. How will you and your team achieve the goals you've decided upon? Procedural conflict can occur because people differ in their ability to see "the big picture." Some team members will see the path clearly from Point A to Point B, others will see only a portion of this path, and still others won't be able to get past the first step. A relationship-based leader believes there is a path between Point A *and* Point B and recognizes that there might be more than one.

For example, your team might be in charge of designing a booth for a local career fair. The construction possibilities are numerous. Writing down the various ideas, collectively deciding on a layout, and delegating jobs to team members keeps the team process flowing. Always keeping the big picture in mind and being open to different processes that might lead you to the goal's achievement will give you the best chance of diminishing procedural conflict.

It is okay for your colleagues and employees to feel passionately about their ideas and perspectives; however, it's not okay to disregard, disrespect, or minimize the ideas and perspectives of the colleagues and employees on your team. This kind of destructive and rude behavior will quickly create a work culture of destructive competition, mistrust, and hostility. The ability to consider, to explore, and to see other team members' perspectives is critical for resolving procedural conflict. Emotional and professional maturity is present when a leader and colleagues can consider, explore, and see other's points of view willingly and respectfully. I wish all adults in the workplace were mature enough to make others feel respected and valued as human beings and professionals. As Aristotle says, "It is the mark of an educated mind to be able to entertain a thought without accepting it."

Interpersonal Conflict

Relationship-based leaders know they cannot legislate or mandate that colleagues and employees "like" one another. However, they can expect colleagues and employees to be professional and work cohesively and respectfully with one another to accomplish the organization's goals. Rarely do team members begin or end their involvement in a team as strangers from one another. They get to know one another well because they interact on a daily or weekly basis. Somewhere in the process, ego, personality differences, personal friction, and work styles emerge. As a team leader, you must maintain a high level of workplace professionalism, no matter what you really *think* or *feel* about the people on your team. Your colleagues and employees will watch to see if you are equitable and fair to all colleagues and employees. If your colleagues and employees know that, in reality, you don't usually see eye-to-eye with one of your team members, but your behavior toward that person is purely professional and even friendly, you have modeled what it means to keep personal differences out of the workplace. Hopefully, they will follow your lead!

I once led a team whose task was to create a public relations booklet outlining the features of an organization. I found myself in the middle of arguments about the order in which each department should be displayed in the booklet. None of the arguments made sense to me until I realized there seemed to be a great deal of animosity between the various department representatives. At that point, I interrupted the conflict by suggesting that departments be showcased in alphabetical order. Only then was the team able to proceed. This is a classic example indicating that, no matter the age, culture, ethnicity, gender, level of education, religious beliefs, or sexual orientation, when personalities conflict and work styles clash, we sometimes forget about professionalism and give in to our personal agendas.

Conflict at the Clinic

The name of the newly-built clinic was the talk of the community because it was captivating, funny, and intriguing: *The Making You Feel Good Clinic*. Everything went well for the first seven years. Then, the clinic hired a new hospital administrator named Florentine Friday, and as with most new leaders, she came in with big, bold, and bright ideas and ideals she wanted to implement immediately. Her ideas and ideals had worked at her previous place of employment.

Florentine Friday was excited about building on the wonderful reputation of *The Making You Feel Good Clinic*. She wanted the clinic to run more effectively and efficiently by improving customer service relations, and she wanted employees to actually spend their working hours performing the work duties for which they were specifically hired. Prior to Florentine Friday coming to the clinic, the clinic's appointment-scheduling procedure was such that any available clinic employee could stop what she or he was doing to assist the patient. This system worked for employees and the patients because patients' needs were met immediately.

Florentine Friday believed there were too many cooks in the kitchen, and she believed this procedure was not the most effective or efficient. She wanted more structure and organization. She wanted the scheduling to be centralized in one area with only receptionists and appointment schedulers setting up patient appointments. She believed errors would be corrected more quickly because fewer people would be involved in the process. She felt the clinic's overall productivity would increase because everyone would be doing the job for which she or he was hired. To her, moving in this direction was a no-brainer, so she was shocked when she got backlash and resistance from the frontline staff (medical assistants, receptionists, and appointment schedulers). They believed *Making You Feel Good's* reputation would be ruined if the customer service experiences that built the clinic's reputation were replaced or eliminated. The frontline staff feared that centralized scheduling would take away from the spontaneous and immediate on-the-spot customer service they provided for their patients. They believed the new system would create longer waiting lines in the clinic and longer waits for telephone call-ins from patients. The frontline staff maintained they were reinforcing and living up to the clinic's original mission. The mission read, "We are here to serve and provide excellent health care services for the needs of our patients while making them happy at the same time."

Here are the four major complaints from the frontline staff:

1. Customer service will become poor and slower.

2. Patients will become unhappy, which will make our jobs difficult.

3. We don't feel empowered anymore to help patients who need us on-the-spot.

4. We won't operate synergistically anymore because appointment scheduling will become centralized.

This conflict created an unpleasant work environment for everyone. Although the doctors, physician assistants, and nurses were not mentioned in the story, they felt the sting of the conflict because the assistants who worked with them began to bring these negative and pessimistic feelings with them to work as they assisted the patients. Here are a few questions for you to ponder as a leader regarding this story:

How should Florentine Friday handle this workplace conflict?

• Is there an idea most viable in this story?

• What is the substantive conflict in the story?

• What is the procedural conflict?

• What is the interpersonal conflict?

• Can Florentine Friday prevent harsh feelings from developing?

• How can Florentine Friday boost team morale if she implements her ideas and disregards the employees' ideas?

THE MAKING OF A WEAK LINK—A CAUSE OF CONFLICT

There's a role-playing activity I use when I present the *Leading with Greatness* workshop, whereby I ask for six audience volunteers to help me illustrate how one person can affect the entire team negatively. There are two responses I receive when I illustrate this candid and real-life activity: people either laugh the entire time, or there is complete silence in the room. I would assume the silence means that I'm hitting home with my example and that people can relate to the activity.

Believe it or not, just one weak link can destroy team morale and erode team unity. It's not hard to know when you have a weak link on your team. *The weak link is that "disturbing person" who, for a variety of reasons, throws off the team's rhythm*—and everyone knows who it is. Knowing who it is, however, isn't as important as understanding *why* this person is creating turbulence and difficulty within the organization. I use the "3 A's" of a Weak Link to sort through and explain the various reasons why the weak link exists in a given team or organization.

The 3 A's of a Weak link

Abilities

For whatever reason, you may be dealing with a colleague or employee who lacks the skills and knowledge necessary for her or his position. The person may be new to the job or may be someone who has chosen to perform at minimum standards, leaving her or him less effective than other members on your team.

© 2003 Ted Goff

"Stop calling me names or I won't find out why your shipment is six months late."

Actions

Not everyone enters a team situation with the same degree of initiative, intensity, and motivation. There will be colleagues or employees who will let you know by their actions or inactions that they would rather be somewhere else. While the words "stubborn" and "lazy" come to mind when thinking of someone who, through action or inaction, is a weak link, I'd like to change the focus instead to the terms "inflexible" and "apathetic." While you may want to initially dismiss a weak link from the team or organization because of their inappropriate actions or inactions, you can give them small and achievable goals—projects where, if they fail to follow through, the team as a whole can pick up the slack. I would say this approach is "pre-termination." Relationship-based leaders assist before they dismiss because there are times when weak links are under-performing for valid reasons, which I'll discuss later.

Attitude

The third reason someone might be a weak link is attitude. The problem with having a negative attitude is that it is horribly infectious. Your attitude always shows as a leader and as an employee. What kind of attitude do you most often show to your colleagues and employees? *Attitude is a person's dominant outlook on life or situations, and is most often communicated non-verbally.* Our attitude is created internally, but others see it externally (remember 93% of face-to-face communication is communicated non-verbally). Our colleagues and employees can tell what we are thinking by observing and watching our facial expressions and body language. Colleagues and employees bringing a negative attitude to the workplace bring with them negative energy that is both counterproductive and disruptive. Sometimes colleagues, employees, and leaders underestimate severely the powerful effects of a bad attitude on a team's performance and productivity.

I interact with 150 college adults and students every week, and I am highly aware of the fact that, as a classroom leader, my emotional state can set either a positive or negative tone for the day. It's a little scary to know that I can bring and transfer negative emotions to my students, and it is pleasing to know that I can also bring and transfer positive energy and emotions to my students. Ask yourself what kind of emotions you bring with you every day to the workplace, and what emotions you pass on to your colleagues and employees. Remember, you play a leading role in creating a friendly, healthy, and welcoming work environment. I guarantee your colleagues and employees will be more effective, efficient, creative, and innovative if their leader creates the kind of work environment they can thrive in comfortably. If not, such a team might eventually fall apart.

Weak links displaying a bad attitude may have a *hidden agenda—a set of personal or private goals that conflict with those of the team or organization.* While a weak link might be effective in other work situations, there may be something about this particular environment contributing to their negative attitude. As a relationship-based leader, try to find out what's happening with the weakest link. Remember that all workplace conflict is the result of an unmet or violated need, want, or expectation. It might be possible to fix the issue easily if you know with whom you're dealing.

To Keep or Not to Keep

Talented international architect Geoff man Kilman had a difficult time accepting direction and feedback from women and people of color in the United States. He was well-liked by the firm's clients, and he contributed immensely to the firm's bottom line, but his negative attitude and actions destroyed team morale and ripped the entire firm apart. As a relationship-based leader, how would you handle Geoff man Kilman's negative attitude? Would you retain, terminate, or suspend him? Would you find another way to handle his behavior? The following section offers a few strategies to help strengthen the weak link on your team.

Supporting and Handling Weak Links Properly

Unfortunately, upon identifying a weak link, most people want to get rid of her or him before they think to offer her or him a professional hand or life jacket. This emotional impulse can be counterproductive to the team as well as potentially harmful or hurtful to the person cited as a weak link. It's important to remember that all weak links are not created equal. Some people behave like weak links intentionally, while others become weak links unintentionally. I call this latter phenomenon the *Situational Weak Link* (those who become legitimate weak links unintentionally). *A Situational Weak Link is someone who becomes a weak link for a brief period of time due to an <u>unfortunate</u> event or situation in her or his life.* Due to unfortunate and unforeseen circumstances, such as deaths, depression, separations, divorces, drug or alcohol-related problems, family issues, sick parents, financial issues, job-related issues, health problems, intimacy issues, or parenting issues, anyone can become a Situational Weak Link.

While I perceive myself as driven, proactive, self-motivated, determined, and tenacious, there are times when I've dropped the ball and haven't followed through on my workplace commitments and expectations. At some point on a scale from 1 to 10—with 10 being the highest ranking and 1 the lowest ranking—we all drop from a 10 to maybe an 8, a 6.5, or even a 3. As driven, self-motivated, proactive, determined, and tenacious as I am, I have been a Situational Weak Link.

I became a Situational Weak Link at Century College between November 27, 2002, and July 1, 2005. It's not that I wasn't producing during this period because if I had not been, I would have been terminated. But I knew that mentally, emotionally, and physically I wasn't operating at optimal peak performance. Those who know me well would probably testify to that statement; I experienced several personal ups and downs during this period. I would like to invite you into my personal and private world to illustrate to you how your personal experiences, like mine, can and will affect professional performance at times. Take a look!

Jermaine's "Situational Weak Link" Timeline

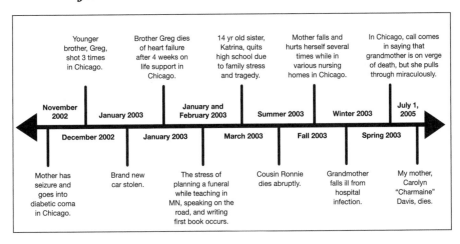

I wish I had the words to articulate how helpless I felt being 400 miles away in St. Paul, MN, when all the various family adversities and challenges took place in Chicago. There were times when I felt emotionally overwhelmed, mentally fatigued, depressed, guilty, confused, helpless, hopeless, and occasionally suicidal. I wanted to just run away from everything; I wanted to go into seclusion and hiding. What's my point? No matter how great a leader, colleague, or employee you may be, when life issues and unforeseen circumstances come your way, you have the potential of turning into a Situational Weak Link. As John Lennon said in the song *Beautiful Boy*, "Life is what happens when you're busy making other plans." I definitely never had any of my family adversities and challenges penciled in my Franklin Covey planner. They *all* came unexpectedly! I was utterly unprepared.

My plans were to be a great college professor, to grow and develop my speaking business, and to become a first-time author. Well, life happened to me, and my productivity subsided. I was fortunate to have the tremendous support of colleagues and peers when I experienced life's difficult moments. I had eight colleagues who rose to the occasion when I needed them most. They would say things like, "Jermaine, I'm here for you if you need me," "What can I do to help you?" "Go home to Chicago," "Don't worry about your exam; I'll proctor your exam for you," and "I'll tape the speeches in your public speaking class for you, so when you return from Chicago, you won't be too far behind in your class schedule." All my colleagues and my dean, Dr. Sue Ehlers, supported me the entire time. Phyllis Hill, an Administrative Assistant in the Humanities Department, was especially thoughtful, sending me supportive e-mails, leaving voice mail messages, and stopping me in the hallways just to check in with me. The colleagues and peers that came through for me were Janet Eyrich, Aaron Klemz, Michele Neaton, Elaine Noel, Allison Searborn, Mark Smeltzer, Pakou Vang, Jon Wendt, and Ida Baltikauskas.

I hope, as a relationship-based leader, you create an environment where colleagues and employees help the weak links before you give up on them or write them off completely. I am so grateful my colleagues helped me when I was at a 3, 5, or 6 at times. I deeply appreciate that they never gave up on me personally and professionally. As a relationship-based leader and a fellow coworker, what do you do when a colleague isn't functioning optimally? Do you provide support, or do you hinder her or him by starting workplace gossip and harboring ill feelings towards her or him? The best way to help a Situational Weak Link is to support her or him personally and professionally.

THE 5 R'S TO HELP WEAK LINKS SUCCEED

Without your active intervention as a relationship-based leader, it's likely that a weak link will become even weaker, and your entire team will suffer. According to Jack Welch, not being fully honest with a weak link regarding their underperformance not only hurts the organization but also the employee's career potential and future. Mr. Welch writes, "Protecting under performers [weak links] always backfires. The worst thing, though, is how protecting people who don't perform hurts the people themselves. The awful thing is that this happens [terminations and layoffs] when the under performers are in their late forties or fifties; they've been carried along for most of their careers. Then suddenly, at an age when starting over can be very tough, they are out of a job with no preparation or planning and a kick in the stomach they may never get over. They feel betrayed, and they should." I encourage using the "5 R's" to attempt to help weak links on your team succeed who are operating at less than their optimal efficiency and maximum productivity.

1) Help them **REFOCUS.**

This process may only take a moment of your time. Taking a team member aside and reminding her or him, clearly, of the upcoming goals and tasks lets her or him know that you care about her or his involvement and that you need her or his active participation in the team. Sometimes colleagues and employees need to be reminded of the tasks for which they were hired. This reminder can take place formally (via quarterly and annual performance reviews) or informally (via e-mails, lunch meetings, and weekly one-on-ones). As a classic example, Tyler, a guy I know, is a network analyst who enjoys working with computers. His job also has a customer service component that he doesn't care to spend much time performing. If his leader reminds him of the dual nature and responsibilities of his goals, job duties, and expectations, Tyler learns from his leader that both components are equally important and need his professional attention.

2) Give them RESOURCES.

We all need certain or specific tools to do our jobs effectively. As relationship-based leaders, we have to ensure our employees are equipped with the necessary tools to fully do their jobs. Leaders always say, "I need you to do this," and the employees say, "That's fine and dandy, but I need this in order to do that for you." It is the leader's job to listen to employees and discover what their needs are so the organization can achieve its goals. Employees need certain dollar amounts, supplies, support systems, and empowerment to achieve workplace goals. The need could be as simple as an access code to the printer, or it could be something more complex, like an updated computer operating system. When employees are fully equipped with the resources to do their jobs, they can deal effectively with difficult and troublesome situations.

Also, in reality, no two team members share the same amount of background information necessary to succeed in the organization. Those who find themselves furthest behind in this area have little to contribute, get bored easily, and lose confidence in their ability to work effectively. Basically, they feel lost. An example would be a team of teachers all teaching the same grade level. If some of the teachers don't have the resources to teach up to benchmark and national standards, they can't be expected to produce top-notch results. By recognizing this situation quickly, you can provide them with adequate resources to catch up with the others and find success as contributing team members.

Real-World Challenge: You lead a team asked to design and create a professional brochure for your company. The software necessary to fulfill the task is familiar to most of the team; however, three members have never used it before. How do you handle this?

3) **RETRAIN** them.

This process, too, involves team members who are out of their element in the team setting due to a lack of adequate skills and information. You can empower such individuals simply by giving them time to acquire the needed skills and to use their newly developed skills and abilities within the organization. In this era of rapid technological advancements and changes, it is not out of the question to retrain your colleagues and employees regularly as new technologies become available.

I was invited to give a speech entitled "Taking Care of Business and Yourself! How to Stay Renewed and Re-energized in Our Fast-paced Work Environments!" for the Tenth Annual Administrative Professional Seminar for Century College and the International Association of Administrative Professionals. What amazed me the most, after I took the stage, was the 150-plus conference participants' enthusiasm. I interrupted my intended introduction to ask the audience why they were so excited about this daylong event, and an over-whelming majority replied, "Our bosses and supervisors are finally investing in us and equipping us to be better employees."

I was ecstatic and happy for them, but I was professionally distraught because I believe employees should never be made to feel that attending company spon-sored workshops, seminars, and training is a privilege. Professional growth and development should be an organizational expectation for all employees. Allowing employees to grow personally and professionally fosters organizational growth! All employees need regular training and retraining so they don't end up

© 2003 Ted Goff

"I'm sorry, everyone in the I Care Department was laid off."

in a professional rut. Maverick organizations and industry leaders who set national and international standards do so because they train and retrain their employees constantly.

I remember when I taught fifth and sixth grade for homeless youth at an elementary school named, "The Learning Center." With a limited budget, Cindy Kelly, the executive director at the time, created a staff development fund of $500 annually for each individual teacher. She told us that $500 was not enough to attend a really good conference, but she wanted her staff to take time off work to train and retrain so we could be the best teachers possible. I think Cindy Kelly understood the connection between training/retraining and organizational growth. Now, that's what I call *Leading with Greatness* through relationship-based leadership!

4) REPOSITION them.

You may have a team member who has remarkable skills and experience in one area but who has been assigned to a task or area in which she or he has no experience or practice. For example, a software developer might find herself shifted, unintentionally, toward a customer service focus. She isn't likely to be a happy employee. Sometimes people are aligned with the right organization, but they may be in the wrong department or position within that organization. In his book, *Now Discover Your Strengths*, Marcus Buckingham forces individuals and organizations to rethink the roles employees play; he proposes organizations can obtain maximum productivity by playing to employees' T.A.G.S. I enjoy the way John C. Maxwell reinforces the power of repositioning for organizational growth and development in *The 17 Indisputable Laws of Teamwork*. "Having the right people in the right places is essential to teambuilding," he writes. "A team's dynamic changes according to the placement of people,"

The Wrong Person in the Wrong Place = Regression.

The Wrong Person in the Right Place = Frustration.

The Right Person in the Wrong Place = Confusion.

The Right Person in the Right Place = Progression.

The Right People in the Right Places = Multiplication.

I've seen the most talented employees become weak links, burn out, and even quit when leaders put them in positions that didn't match their T.A.G.S. As a relationship-based leader, you must play to their T.A.G.S. Great athletic coaches position their players according to their greatest T.A.G.S. to ensure success, so great leaders should play people to their T.A.G.S. (Talents, Abilities, Gifts, and Skills).

5) REMOVE, REPLACE, or RETIRE them.

Clearly this option is the last resort. If you sense a team member really doesn't want to be there or if you realize her or his skills will not benefit the rest of the team, there is no point in letting everyone suffer. You need to appropriately pass that person on to some other area where they are a better fit so that the rest of the team can maintain its maximum synergy, productivity, and morale. The person you want to remove may not be completely useless within the organizational setting; it is possible that she or he is simply not a match for your team and is better suited for another area. I know removing, replacing, and retiring an individual is easier said than done, especially with organizational bureaucracy, politics, rules, regulations, and union issues. Here's what I *do* know about maintaining the presence of weak links within organizations: they can develop attitudes, behaviors, and work styles that will begin to affect entire departments—and negative departments are known to erode organizations. My suggestions involve putting people on work performance plans to improve work performance; please consult your company's human resources office and legal team as to how to effectively deal with an under performing weak link. Make sure you document all observations of the weak link's inabilities to perform expected work duties, and follow your company's rules and regulations regarding documentation. Most importantly, as a relationship-based leader, behave ethically and professionally throughout the entire process.

Real-World Challenge: As head of the creative division of your company, you were forced to let someone go for stealing. No one else knows the reason he was fired. What do you say to the team when you meet again?

THE 4 CONFLICT RESOLUTION METHODS

Can a leader's ability to resolve conflict effectively create a healthy and safe workplace in which its employees thrive? Absolutely! Can a leader's inability to resolve conflict effectively contribute to a negative, unhealthy, and unsafe workplace for its employees? Absolutely! I want to be clear about my perspective. I'm not saying colleagues and employees don't contribute to negative, unhealthy, and unsafe work environments. They definitely do. This book is about how to effectively lead with greatness by being a relationship-based leader; what I'm trying to convey is that colleagues and employees look to their leaders to lead them through the tough and terrible terrains of team and organizational conflict. Leaders who avoid, deny, and minimize conflict contribute to a negative, unhealthy, unwelcoming, and unsafe workplace.

It is important for all employees of an organization to be trained in emotional intelligence and successful conflict resolution methods. Why? Because workplace violence is on the rise. If workers and leaders are not emotionally intelligent when dealing with arguments, disagreements, and disputes, their emotions can easily become negative, destructive, and violent (because they left their base-line). The U.S. Centers for Disease Control and Prevention (CDC) and the National Institute for Occupational Safety and Health (NIOSH) state, "1.7 million workers are injured every year in non-fatal workplace assaults." Unresolved conflicts, misplaced emotions, and resentful feelings towards colleagues and leaders can lead to verbal aggression, emotional abuse, and physical violence. Reports from the CDC revealed between the years of 1993 and 1999, "Over 800 workplace homicides per year were recorded by the Bureau of Labor Statistics' Census of Fatal Occupational Injuries." They also stated, "According to recent data, 677 workplace homicides occurred in 2000." Here's what's best about the CDC's and NIOSH's proactive suggestion, "Training employees in nonviolent response and conflict resolution has been suggested to reduce the risk that violatile situations will escalate to physical violence. Training should not be regarded as the sole prevention strategy but as a component in a comprehensive approach to reducing workplace violence." Proactive organizations and teams nip destructive conflict in the bud before it escalates and gets out of control.

Bottom-line: You can't lead with greatness without being able to resolve team and organizational conflict effectively when it arises. *Conflict resolution is the process of resolving an argument or disagreement by achieving mutual satisfaction for everyone involved in the conflict.* Leaders are organizational firefighters. As long as companies still hire human beings to achieve company goals, leaders will need to address difficult and painful conflicts. Colleagues and employees expect leaders to extinguish company fires competently and effectively; those fires include angry and emotional outbursts, verbal explosions, toxic gossip, physical intimidation, and inappropriate team conflict. If leaders can't extinguish these company fires, employees will begin to ask one another, "What the heck is she or he in a leadership position for?" They will say, "Isn't that a part of their job? To make it a safe workplace for us?"

No need to fear or fret—this next section will equip you with the two best approaches for addressing, confronting, and dealing effectively with team and organizational conflict. Pay close attention to the two approaches of conflict resolution (lose-lose and win-lose) to avoid at all times if you want to lead with greatness. Think about how each conflict resolution method could possibly *help* or *hinder* your team or organization from growing and developing exponentially. If you find managing team and organizational conflict a difficult task, try using the following ten questions as conversation starters suggested by Michael Marquart in his book *Leading with Questions:*

1. How can we separate the people from the problem—diagnose the cause of the conflict?

2. What does each side want?

3. Do all sides have a clear understanding of the issues?

4. How can I encourage them to view the conflict from the other side's perspective and to practice active listening?

5. What are the common areas of interest?

6. How can each side get what it wants?

7. What are the issues that are incompatible between the two sides?

8. What are the most important goals of each side?

9. What objective criteria will we use as a basis for our decisions?

10. How can we disagree in an agreeable fashion?

Low Levels of Conflict Resolution (Avoid these at all cost)
Lose-lose

The lose-lose conflict resolution method occurs when all parties involved believe and feel their needs, wants, and expectations were unmet. Conflicts ending in a lose-lose situation are a result of professionally immature, narrow-minded, self-ish, and stubborn leaders and employees who refuse to see other people's points of view on an issue. When leaders, colleagues, and employees refuse to explore other ideas and opinions, the lose-lose situation is unavoidable. Nobody leaves this kind of conversation or interaction happy. Each party feels they've given too much towards the conflict resolution and have not gained any satisfaction in return. Each person involved will have a difficult time moving forward, so future problems with pessimism, negative attitudes, low productivity, low morale, and spiteful feelings can result.

Imagine a situation in which you and your colleagues differ on an important workplace issue and don't choose to agree to disagree. Maybe we don't even con-sider the option of exploring and understanding each other's position. This can leave both of us feeling angry, frustrated, unheard, motionless with the task still at hand, and lacking a practical resolution. A lose-lose resolution undermines and tears apart the trust built between the leader and her or his colleagues and employees, and it can destroy the leader's credibility. A lose-lose resolution can also stagnate or stop progression towards the company and team goals.

Win-lose

"It's my way or the highway." This statement, which represents many people's beliefs, gives birth to the win-lose conflict resolution method and is the child of hubris. An organization is doomed when leaders and teammates believe everything must go their way. When a win-lose culture is embedded within the organizational fabric, the atmosphere will be filled with anxiety, tension, and unnecessary stress. I've heard some colleagues and employees describe a win-lose atmosphere as if they're walking on eggshells because, if they disagree with a leader, they never know the final outcome of their honest dialogue and open communication (honest and open communication is honorable but can also be risky).

Technically, *win-lose situations involve at least one happy and satisfied party, but conflict resolution involving a winner and a loser still leaves one party utterly unhappy and dissatisfied.* How much does an angry, bitter, and resentful colleague or employee cost a company on a daily or weekly basis? A conflict ending with a win-lose resolution will inevitably strain the team's performance, productivity, and profits. As a relationship-based leader, you need to prevent win-lose conflicts to avoid team members choosing sides.

Let's say my team and I have the task of choosing between two telephone systems offered to our organization. The team is at a stalemate and asks for more information regarding each telephone system. As their team leader, I make it clear to my colleagues and employees which telephone system I like better. Rather than providing the information my team members requested, I make a final decision and select the telephone system I favor without considering my colleagues' and employees' preferences and recommendations. Will my colleagues and employees feel I've betrayed them? Absolutely! Will there now be animosity between my team and I? You better believe it! Will they trust me in the future, or have I burned my professional bridges as a leader? Bridge, what bridge?

Leaders who abuse their power in this fashion get what they want, but lose credibility and the ability to motivate, inspire, and influence others in the process. In this example, all parties should've had a fair opportunity to explain why they believed one telephone system was more preferable for the organization's telecommunications needs. The leader may have gotten what she or he wanted but, again, at what expense? Can this leader move a company effectively toward goals when she or he resolves conflict with a win-lose mentality? Probably not!

High Levels of Conflict Resolution (Use these often)
Compromise

Compromise is clearly a step up from the two types of conflict resolution methods we've just discussed. *In a true compromise, all parties give up and sacrifice*
something they desire with the goal and hope of obtaining something they desire
more. Each team member knows she or he has given up something in the process,
and colleagues and employees can feel resentful if they perceive the compromise
as an unfair process. However, partial satisfaction may be all you can get when
you shuffle through various organizational issues. Using the telephone system
example, suppose that the leader provided the team with the information necessary to reach a well-informed decision. Team members might identify and discuss
each phone system's positive, negative, and neutral features and then render a
decision through the give-and-take process.

Many perfectly-adequate team decisions are made this way. Many people and
organizations use this method because it seems relatively fair, just, and equitable.
Everyone gets a little piece of what she or he wants, and compromise appears to
go faster when teams and organizations are trying to reach a decision quickly.
Willingness to compromise and a consistency of fairness upholds and reinforces a
leader's character and credibility and maintains a relationship-based leadership

role. In many cases, compromise can show that a leader listens to and cares about their colleagues' and employees' ideas and opinions. However, when issues or topics are core values for a colleague or employee, be prepared, as a relationship-based leader, to experience silence, resistance, push back, or complete shutdown if you ask for a compromise. Leaders must then decide what's really best for the overall organization and its members. Employees must decide if the organization's mission and values align with her or his personal and professional values and convictions. Some people decide to leave an organization when they feel its values conflict with their own. I see this as a productive outcome for both parties because neither has to resent her or his personal and professional values being challenged, disrespected, or violated. You have to do what's best for you mentally, emotionally, physically, professionally, and spiritually. You must be able to sleep at night with the compromises you've made. So, compromise strategically and wisely!

Win-win

The win-win conflict resolution method occurs when all parties involved in a disagreement or dispute feel satisfied with the outcome of the conflict because their needs, wants, and expectations were fully achieved. While this is obviously the ideal goal, a win-win solution does not come easily and often involves lengthy dialogue, discussion, and respectful debate. It's tempting to decide not to sacrifice the time required for win-win resolution, but I assure you that the time and energy is well worth the final outcome. Parties leaving a win-win situation do so with the satisfaction of knowing they were mutually understood; they retain respect for the other party and have a greater commitment to the project and organization's success. A friend of mine, Lynne, emerged from conflict with her boss in a win-win situation. She had been struggling with her job and feeling bored, undervalued, and resentful of the work she was doing. She approached her leader, who had noticed her poor productivity, loss of enthusiasm, and low team morale. A discussion ensued; Lynne confessed her dissatisfaction with her current position although she was afraid of being professionally reprimanded, demoted, or fired. She was amazed when her leader listened to her, understood how she felt, and instead of letting her go, allowed and encouraged her to transfer laterally to a position in which she felt much happier and connected professionally.

THE BOTTOM LINE OF CONFLICT RESOLUTION AND *LEADING WITH GREATNESS*

The win-win and compromise resolutions are almost always possible if leaders and employees follow my suggestions for building, creating, and earning trust within their teams and organizations. It's mentally and emotionally easier to argue, debate, and disagree with those you trust professionally. If colleagues and employees believe and trust their leaders, constructive criticisms will not be misconstrued or taken out of context, and employees will be more likely to engage in honest dialogue and open communication.

The last thing a colleague or employee wants is to be perceived as a cynic, whiner, or complainer when they've simply provided honest feedback. If more relationship-based leaders and employees took heed of my suggestions written in part three—on apologizing using the 5 Steps to Regaining Trust when they'd offended, wounded, or wronged a teammate—then high levels of conflict resolution (compromise and win-win) would be used more often in resolving team conflicts. Trust, respect, and open-mindedness are absolute prerequisites for resolving conflict in a healthy and effective manner. Author of *The Five Dysfunctions of a Team*, Patrick Lencioni, describes the relationship between trust and teamwork when he writes, "Trust lies at the heart of a functioning, cohesive team. Without it, teamwork is all but impossible. Trust is the foundation of real teamwork." Simply put, teams and organizations cannot resolve conflicts without having a high trust culture where people feel safe sharing their true ideas and opinions.

Constructive conflict and healthy team debate is possible when all leaders, colleagues, and employees trust one another. Lacking such team trust, conflicts are usually resolved with lose-lose and win-lose methods. Without team trust, colleagues and employees will not be fully honest and open due to fear of career punishment and retaliation from leaders and teammates. A relationship-based leader simply cannot cultivate the necessary relationships to lead with greatness when trust is absent.

You've seen how I divided the four methods of conflict resolutions into two categories: low levels of conflict resolution, which are lose-lose and win-lose, and high levels of conflict resolution, which are compromise and win-win. Even though I've described the four conflict resolution methods, please understand that all four methods are not capable of significantly reducing or completely eliminating workplace conflict. Let me explain. Whether I'm speaking at a conference with thousands of audience members or working one-on-one in a coaching session with a leader, I never, and I mean *never*, suggest resolving conflicts with lose-lose or win-lose. I couldn't have written *Leading with Greatness* with conviction and integrity if I supported either of the lower levels of conflict resolution. A person cannot be a relationship-based leader possessing a lose-lose or win-lose paradigm. I encourage relationship-based leaders who want to lead with greatness during conflict to seek a win-win resolution or, if all else fails, to pursue a compromise. I advocate for win-win as the best approach for resolving individual, team, and workplace conflict. However, in the "real world" where some leaders, colleagues, and employees might be arrogant, inconsiderate, narrow-minded, selfish, and stubborn, compromise may be the best approach to resolving conflict during difficult dialogue, controversial conversations, and strict deadlines. Win-win and compromise are high levels of conflict resolution that enable and encourage team members to seek, consider, explore, and evaluate alternative ideas and solutions. High-level conflict resolution grows, develops, and moves individuals, teams, and, ultimately, organizations, from chaos and conflict to communication and cooperation.

Final Thoughts on *Leading with Greatness!*

I began to develop the theories and practical ideas outlined in this book in my early twenties when I taught homeless youth in downtown Minneapolis. During this time when I taught at-risk and disadvantaged youth, I quickly learned that no significant learning takes place until you first establish a meaningful interpersonal relationship with the people you lead. I discovered and developed my philosophy of relationship-based leadership which contends that a leader deliberately establishes and builds interpersonal relationships with colleagues and employees before attempting to lead them. The youth I worked with for three years were accustomed to inconsistency and unpredictability from the adults in their lives. When students entered my classroom, I could sense an air of apathy, fear, hesitation, and uncertainty. I saw the physical manifestation of defensive postures and cautious demeanors, and I felt an invisible fence of guarded communication due to the defensive walls they had constructed to protect their emotions from potential agony, pain, and hurt.

The students that entered my classroom were already behind two to three years academically due to the unstable homes and school environments in which they lived and operated. When I looked at all the variables in the equation, I realized they did not trust me, and I knew I had to build and create a healthy and trusting environment before I could reach, relate to, and teach these students. When I began to create a trusting environment, they could listen to me, and I could then pursue the opportunity to teach them. I believe the same principle I used then applies to everyday workplace situations. I believe leaders should adopt and apply the paradigm that no significant motivation, inspiration, or influence can occur until you first establish a significant interpersonal relationship with the people you lead. Relationship-based leadership is all about establishing significant interpersonal relationships with colleagues and employees before trying to lead them toward accomplishing organizational goals.

The theories and practical ideas I learned while working with at-risk youth were tested when I began my marketing and sales career with a Fortune 500 snack food company. I knew relationship-based teaching and leadership worked well with youth, but I still had to test the consistency of my ideas. I tested my knowledge and ideas when I worked with college-educated professionals twice my age and with those having more professional work experience than me. Hired at the age of twenty-two, I was a young black man from inner-city Chicago, living and working in northern Minnesota and Wisconsin. I was fresh out of graduate school when I inherited a team of fifteen route sales associates as a district manager trainee. I was excited about my new career, but I rapidly discovered that my fifteen sales associates were angry with the company and envious and resentful toward me because I was hired into a leadership role "solely due to my formal education" (so they believed). I knew that the company was moving in a new direction with their recruiting, hiring, and promotion practices. They wanted talented people in leadership positions, so they had begun to build a stronger organization by promoting homegrown talent from within, recruiting great talent from outside, and recruiting talented young people just out of graduate school.

When I realized my new team of fifteen sales associates didn't share a mutual excitement about my new role or the company's new direction, I was initially overcome with fear. That fear stemmed from multiple factors including my age, my race, my culture, and the geographic location from which I came. Along with my concerns about the team adapting to the new organizational shifts, I worried whether I could motivate, inspire, and influence a homogenous team and if they could embrace a leader bringing in new forms of diversity. I quickly had to learn how to connect with my team, to overcome my fears, and to reach my annual goal of $6 million in snack food sales with a team, as I learned from a district manager, was secretly envious and resentful of me. I began my new leadership position humbly and started to establish interpersonal relationships with each of the fifteen sales associates I was responsible for leading and guiding.

When I built and created a healthy and trusting work environment for everyone to thrive in, my job as a leader became easier. Now, I'm not saying that everyone was on board immediately or that being a newly-appointed leader was a piece of cake, because it wasn't. However, I knew and was convinced that I could not motivate, inspire, or influence my sales team towards the $6 million departmental goal if I did not establish significant interpersonal relationships with each of them.

At the beginning of this text, I asked if you thought leaders were born with natural leadership attributes or if leaders could be cultivated by receiving adequate training, practice, and direction. I hope you chose the latter because, at any point in your career, that leader could be you.

I hope you've learned that *Leading with Greatness* is relationship-driven. I illustrated what it takes to be a great leader and how to lead by motivating, inspiring, and influencing your colleagues and employees. I hope that you discovered that a significant part of leadership involves cheering and guiding your colleagues and employees toward greatness and how important it is to them to be seen by you as competent, significant, and valuable. We talked about how to build your credibility as a leader. I hope you walk away with the belief that being a great leader means setting a good example, which includes apologizing for your unthinkable actions ***and*** behaving your way out of your mistakes when you have offended colleagues and employees.

I also hope you found a leadership style that is a perfect fit for you and your situation. Perhaps you were able to find out what T.A.G.S. (Talents, Abilities, Gifts, and Skills) you have and how they do or don't match those of your colleagues and employees. Can you now answer the following questions with clarity and conviction: Did you find out your company's or organization's mission statement? Did you find out your company's vision and how it applies to your leadership vision? Did you find out your company's goals and how they apply to your leadership goals? Do you now know how to incorporate the purpose, vision, and goals of your organization into everything you do?

What about your communication style? Often, people nag and complain about the others' communication, but it takes a great leader to be critical of her or his own style and to attempt to make positive changes in how she or he connects with and relates to others on her or his team. Are you in tune with your base-line when you communicate? Can you see how your body talk informs you of how to communicate when you are agitated or stressed?

Finally, I walked you through the delicate balance of conflict—how to handle difficult and complicated situations in an environment where lots of personalities are enmeshed and how hubris or a simple unmet or violated need, want, or expectation can sometimes be the greatest barrier to resolving personal and organizational conflict. I hope you can walk away with practical strategies of dealing with different types of conflict as well as an understanding of the value of conflict resolution. As a relationship-based leader, perhaps you realized that the same relationships you have with your colleagues and employees in good times will help you also in the difficult times.

I am blessed with the wonderful opportunity to travel the globe teaching and sharing the ideas, strategies, and solutions outlined here. Writing *Leading with Greatness* wasn't originally a top priority for me, but I knew I needed to complete it. This book was finally birthed because so many workshop participants continuously encouraged—and sometimes pressured—me to turn the workshop materials into a book so that they could relive the powerful content and apply it to their jobs and daily lives. I wrote this book with the authentic desire to assist leaders in moving their people and organizations forward, and used the philosophy of what I affectionately call ***relationship-based leadership*** as the core foundation.

Whether you strive for leadership or whether the opportunity presents itself to you unexpectedly, you should now understand the complexities, challenges, and rewards of such a position. Nobody but *you* can turn *you* into an effective leader who leads with greatness. If you choose to lead to succeed, that success will reflect both on your character and abilities and also on the outcome of any leadership task you assume. Your ability to cultivate, nurture, and build strong relationships with your colleagues and employees will be the magnet that draws your team together and which provides the impetus for them to feel the same success you feel in yourself. The journey and quest of learning to lead with greatness is never an easy exploration. *Leading with Greatness* requires physical stamina, emotional tenacity, and mental fortitude. Good success to you and many blessings on your journey and quest to *Leading with Greatness!*

BIOGRAPHY

Jermaine M. Davis

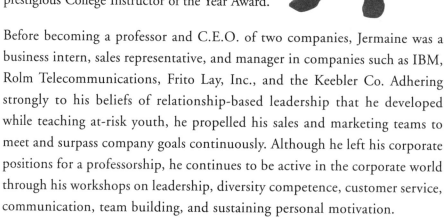

Jermaine M. Davis is the author of four books including the successful seller; *Get Up Off Your Butt & Do It NOW! Staying Motivated Even When You Don't Feel Like It.* He is one of the country's most requested speakers and teachers in the areas of customer service, diversity competence, leadership, motivation, team building, overcoming adversity, and organizational communication. Jermaine is C.E.O. and founder of Seminars & Workshops, Inc. and Snack Attack Vending of Minnesota. He is a professor of Communication Studies at Century College in Minnesota and was nominated by students and presented with the prestigious College Instructor of the Year Award.

Before becoming a professor and C.E.O. of two companies, Jermaine was a business intern, sales representative, and manager in companies such as IBM, Rolm Telecommunications, Frito Lay, Inc., and the Keebler Co. Adhering strongly to his beliefs of relationship-based leadership that he developed while teaching at-risk youth, he propelled his sales and marketing teams to meet and surpass company goals continuously. Although he left his corporate positions for a professorship, he continues to be active in the corporate world through his workshops on leadership, diversity competence, customer service, communication, team building, and sustaining personal motivation.

Jermaine is a Chicago native and presently lives in St. Paul, MN.

A Special Invitation from the Author

If you are interested in bringing Jermaine M. Davis to your organization or school for a book signing, or to learn more about products, other available workshops, and discounts on orders of 10 or more copies of *Leading with Greatness!*, please contact our corporate office at:

Phone: (651) 487-7576
Email: jermaine@jermainedavis.com
Website: www.jermainedavis.com

To find out about our discount program for resellers of *Leading with Greatness!*, please contact our marketing and sales department at (651) 487-7576 or (773) 936-0222.

Here are the best ways Jermaine can help your organization succeed:

• Keynote and Endnote Presentations

• Executive and Managerial Coaching

• Public Speaking Coaching

• New Employee and Student Orientation Training

• Affinity and Employee Resource Group Training

• Faculty and Professional Staff Development Programs

• New Supervisor Coaching and Training

• Professional Association Conferences

• Parents' Day Programs

• Board of Director Training

• Teacher In-services

• Holiday Celebrations

• Award and Banquet Celebrations

• Student Leadership and Team Building Training

• Full-and Multi-Day Residencies

• Hall Directors and Residential Assistant Training

• Greek Life: Fraternity and Sorority Workshops

• Spiritual and Religious Conferences and Retreats

• Dr. Martin Luther King, Jr., Celebrations

• Diversity and Multicultural Celebrations and Events